SECURE THE KNOT

Build And Strengthen Your Marriage Bond

✳ ✳ ✳

It is narrated that Aisha [R.A] asked the Prophet [S.A.W]:
"How is your love for me?" The Prophet [S.A.W] replied :
"Like the rope`s knot."
(To signify that the love was strong and secure.)
Every so often after that, she would ask him,
"How is the knot?" and he would reply
"the same as ever."
[reported in Hiya al Awliya]

Dedication

بِسْمِ اللَّهِ الرَّحْمَنِ الرَّحِيمِ
In the name of Allaah, the most Gracious, the most Merciful.
All praises and thanks are due to Allaah, the Lord of the worlds. We worship Him, we praise Him and we seek His Guidance.

Abu Darda reported that the Messenger of Allaah [S.A.W] said; "No Muslim servant supplicates for his brother behind his back but that the angel says: And for you the same." [Ṣaḥīḥ Muslim 2732]

In light of the above-mentioned Hadeeth, I would like to take this opportunity to request that you join me in making a sincere supplication to Allaah.

Yaa Allaah! send down Your Mercy and Assistance to those who defend Your cause, and upon my mother Maryam, my father Jamil, my sister Rasheedah, and all of my family. And also upon all the Muslimeen and their families. Aameen.

SECURE THE KNOT

CONTENTS

Preface

"And among His signs is this; that He created for you mates from among yourselves, that ye may dwell with them in tranquility. And He has put love and mercy between your [hearts]. Verily in that are signs for those who reflect. [Ar Rum 30:21]

Three days are of utmost significance in the life of every man and woman. The first is the day of birth, the second is the day of marriage, and the third is the day of death. In this book that you hold in your hands, we will be focusing on the events that follow the second day - the day that you will marry. This is the day that you will become the other half to someone else whilst simultaneously completing half of your own deen. Let me bring to your attention the well known Hadeeth where the Prophet Muhammad [S.A.W] said "Whoever Allaah provides with a righteous wife, Allaah has assisted him in half of his religion...." [al-Mu'jam al-Awsaṭ 992 Sahih according to Al-Suyuti] This Hadeeth, along with many others, highlights the significance of marriage in Islam. We therefore must put great effort into educating ourselves about marriage so that we are well prepared for this incredible chapter of our lives.

A successful marriage is precious, and just like everything that is precious in this world, you have to work hard to attain it. There is a famous saying that "if you fail to prepare, you prepare to fail". Unfortunately, as a Muslim ummah, we are failing greatly when it comes to preparing for marriage and educating about it. It is no surprise then, that divorce rates within the Muslim community continue to rise at an alarming rate.

Oftentimes when marriage is spoken about, we do not delve deep into the topic and explore how it really is to be married on a day-to-day basis. We do not put much importance on the topic of building a romantic connection within the marriage. In fact, if we are to speak honestly, most of the marriage advice that is given within our communities is geared towards the Muslim woman – teaching her how to be the perfect, submissive wife. And the Muslim man? Well, he is often only taught about his rights and very little about his responsibilities within a marriage.

Do we forget that marriage takes equal effort from both parties in order for it to be successful? We must put effort into teaching our women how to be good wives and equally our men how to be good husbands. We must teach our women their rights within an Islamic marriage so that they are able to defend these rights, should these be abused.

The lack of correct marriage preparation has had devastating consequences for the Muslim community. I use the harsh word devastating because how else would you describe being in an unhappy, loveless marriage for years or even decades? Or how else would you describe divorce? Divorce leaves families broken, it leaves single parents struggling with poverty, it leaves children to be raised without their father or mother. And possibly the worst thing that divorce does is that it steals from the eman of so many of our sisters. It is no secret that so many of our sisters begin to lower their eman after going through a divorce. This is devastating and we must do better as a community to provide education and support.

We must look deeper within our communities to find out the cause of this high level of divorce or why there are so many unhappy homes. The truth is that seldom does divorce happen spontaneously. It is usually the culmination of minor issues that are left to fester over time. These minor issues could possibly have been resolved had the couple had the knowledge on how to build a solid connection, how to communicate effectively, and how to understand each other well.

Aside from the devastating consequences of divorce, another consequence of failing to prepare well for marriage is that it can be difficult to know how to build a solid and genuine connection with your spouse. This can then lead to a loveless, unhappy marriage. This is where the couple remains in an unhappy marriage just so that they satisfy cultural norms and avoid bringing shame on the family by divorcing. Or they may remain married just for the sake of the children. Staying married for the sake of the children is never encouraged. Children are able to sense their parents` unhappiness and they too will not be truly happy. Studies have shown that the long-term effects of children growing up in such households are catastrophic. Perhaps some may even argue that a loveless marriage is worse than a divorce.

It is important to be aware that even though a marriage starts with just two people, the effects of it are felt by many others. Most importantly, the children that you will bear. Those children will look up to you and they will learn from you consciously and subconsciously. From watching the two of you together, they will learn what to expect from marriage and how they should behave, not just in marriage but in everyday life. Families are what make a community, and marriage is the start of a family. If our marriages are weak, so will our community be weak. This is why It is so important that we make our marriages succeed and flourish.

A Hadeeth that emphasises the importance of marriage was reported by Jabir who said that the Messenger of Allaah, [SAW] said, "Verily, Satan places his throne over the water and he sends out his troops. The closest to him in rank are the greatest at causing tribulations. One of them says: I have done this and this.

Satan says: You have done nothing. Another one says: I did not leave this man alone until I separated him from his wife. Satan embraces him and he says: You have done well.". Ṣaḥīḥ Muslim 2813. We learn from this Hadeeth that the devil is most pleased when a man and his wife separate. Why do we think this is? Because he knows the lasting and devastating effects that this can have on the Muslim community as a whole.

It is for the reasons mentioned above that I am compelled to write this book. In this book that you hold in your hands, we will do our best to guide you using evidence from the Quran and authentic Sunnah on how to build a beautiful bond with your spouse. You will find many examples and direct guidance on what to do to help you achieve this. We have explored everything in great detail. This book is suitable for those who are searching for a spouse to get married to, for those who are newly wedded, and for those who have been married for many many years. It is never too late to build a strong bond in your marriage or to rekindle a bond that may have been lost or was never there to begin with. This book will, by the leave of Allaah, help you to understand how to build a thriving marriage, help you to become a better person, and you may find that it also teaches you a thing or two about yourself.

In different places within the book, the author may appear to be referring to the wife or the husband specifically. This is to facilitate in building a realistic scenario and is helpful when examples are given. Please note that the lesson being given is directed to both the husband and the wife always, even though we may mention only one. At certain times, it may appear that the author is putting blame on the husband or on the wife. This is not the case, rather it is because some matters relate more to the wife and others more to the husband.

✳ ✳ ✳

1. Introduction

Marriage is amongst the greatest of blessings that Allaah has bestowed upon us. In Islam, marriage is considered as an act of worship. This means that you get rewarded for everything that you do within your marriage. Even small acts like smiling at your spouse or giving a compliment are rewarded. Getting married is strongly encouraged in Islam. The Messenger of Allah [S.A.W] said: "Marriage is part of my sunnah, and whoever does not follow my sunnah has nothing to do with me. Get married, for I will boast of your great numbers before the nations..... (Sunan ibn Majah 1846)

In the era that we live in today, it is normal for a couple to be in a courtship for a number of years before they finally decide to get married. This is the complete opposite of Islamic teachings. In Islam, there is to be no private communication between a man and a woman before they marry. There must always be a third party present with them at all times. This third party is known as the wali. There are to be no private phone conversations, not even text messages between the two without the presence of the wali. It is only after the nikah has been pronounced and they have become husband and wife that they may be alone without a third party. Now, whilst that process may seem strange to many of us who have grown up in different societies, there is actually so much beauty and wisdom in the Islamic marriage process. This process allows for the couple to first get to know each other on a deeper level without lust or desires crowding their judgment. It also allows for a build up of excitement as two families prepare to become one. Studies have shown that marriages that begin this way last longer than those that begin with courting.

Marriage is at the forefront of the mind of every Muslim. The thought of marriage brings much excitement and eagerness. Many a number of hours are spent by young ladies discussing their ideal husband, the colour of the wedding gown they will wear, and the names that they will give to their future children. However, the idea of marriage may also bring with it a hidden worry. The worry about the marriage itself. What will happen once all the festivities are over and real life begins? Who is this new person that you are going to spend the rest of your life with? Will you have a connection with them? How do you even begin to navigate this exponential part of your life?

For many Muslims, marriage will be the first time that they will spend time alone with somebody from the opposite gender. It will be the very first time that they experience a romantic relationship and so it can be a nerve-wracking time, understandably. Unfortunately, many of us will enter into marriage being ill-equipped and unprepared.

Anybody can have a marriage - but a beautiful, thriving marriage is something rare. This is the type of marriage where your husband will be able to say to people years later that by Allaah! he has never been given anything better than you! Or maybe the type of marriage where even years later, your husband is still brought to tears just by hearing the voice of your sister as she reminds him of you. This was the type of marriage that our beloved Prophet [SAW] and Khadijah [R.A] had. This is the type of love and rahma that we all want to enjoy. This type of marriage is definitely something that can be achieved by any one of us. However, it will not appear magically overnight. You will need to, first of all, ask Allaah for His blessings, and then "tie your camel" by working hard to achieve this type of marriage. Are you ready to put in the work?

As Muslims, we are so often misunderstood by the whole world. We often find it difficult to fit into society due to ignorance and prejudice from others. That is why we so desperately need our marriages to be places of peace and love and a sanctuary from the cruel cold world.

Now picture this; It is the day of your walima - the day has gone well, Alhamdulillah! The food was delicious and everything went as planned. You looked good, your spouse looked great, and you are so very happy. You are now husband and wife and all of a sudden, just like that, you are alone with each other for the first time. For many Muslim ladies and gents, this will be the first time ever for them to be alone in the presence of someone from the opposite gender. The atmosphere is filled with nervousness, awkwardness, and excitement! Nobody knows what to do or say. Que the awkward laughs and coughs as you try your best to avoid eye contact. Believe it or not, this is actually a very precious moment. This is exactly how Allaah has decreed it to be. It is within this shyness and excitement that you have a clean slate to start something beautiful. It is during this moment of beautiful vulnerability that you are able to form a special bond that is unique to the two of you.

Although nobody can fully prepare you for that exact moment, in this book, we will strive to help you become aware of the needs and emotions of your spouse so that you can have the right foundations to build a beautiful marriage. How beautiful is life when you find somebody who truly loves you and understands you for who you are? The Messenger of Allah [S.A.W] said, "The world is enjoyment and the best enjoyment in the world is a righteous wife." (Sahih Muslim 1467). This Hadith shows us that an enjoyable marriage really can be the greatest joy in this world.

You must be prepared to put in the effort and time required to achieve a strong marriage bond. The beautiful thing about marriage is that the effort that you put in will soon become second nature to you and you won't even have to think about it. So do not feel overwhelmed, instead, be prepared to improve yourself.

Too often, we hear the excuse "that is just the way that I am, I cannot change". This is untrue, we are all able to unlearn negative ways and habits and stop them from ruining our future prospects and hurting those whom we love. It is crucial that you have an open mind and that you are prepared to make changes to be a better person for yourself and your spouse.

As you read through this book, it is empirical that you examine yourself and your character specifically. Be prepared to note your own shortcomings, to be self critical, and to improve.

* * *

2. Difficulty Forming A Bond

B efore we begin to discus about how to form a bond in your marriage, we must first be aware of the things that may make it difficult to form a strong marriage bond. Sometimes these causes may be insidious, and we might even be completely unaware of them. The three things to be discussed are cultural exploitations, past trauma, and low self-esteem. It is important that these issues are acknowledged and discussed early on in the marriage and perhaps even before marriage.

When a man and a woman get married, Allaah places between them love and mercy. Allaah says in the Holy Qur`an "And among His Signs is this, that He created for you mates from among yourselves, that ye may dwell in tranquillity with them, and He has put love and mercy between your (hearts): verily in that are Signs for those who reflect." Ar Rum 30:21. This Ayat tells us that Allaah places love and mercy between spouses after the marriage. Often times you may hear people say that after the nikah was performed, they felt "different" or they felt at ease - as if they have known this person all their life. This is from the mercy of Allaah that He places between the husband and wife. It is important to acknowledge any previously deeper-rooted issues such as those we will discuss, so that we allow the love and mercy to develop well.

Cultural Exploitation

It is a blessing from Allaah that He has created us with many different cultures. This makes it interesting for us to get to know each other. As Allaah says in the Glorious Qur'an "O mankind! Behold, We have created you all out of a male and a female, and have made you into nations and tribes so that you might come to know one another. " Al Hujurat 49:13. There are many aspects of culture that are great! For example, the emphasis on respect for the elderly or the great focus on maintaining the bonds within a community. However, there are also many damaging cultural practices that can play a part in hindering you from forming a strong and loving bond in your marriage. Many cultural practices have no basis in the Quran and Sunnah. Instead, they were invented by people a long time ago, and truth be told, most of them are oppressive to women.

An example of a toxic cultural practice is that In some cultures, women are not allowed to speak freely with their husbands. They must simply listen and obey and have no opinions of their own even if the husband is in the wrong. How can you expect to form a bond of love and trust with a person if you are not allowed to even express yourself freely? When we teach women to be afraid of their husbands, we automatically stop the marriage from being an honest and safe place. When a woman does not feel safe in her husband's love, she can never fully let go of her inhibitions and shyness in order to be the best version of herself.

In Islam, we are taught that the wife must obey her husband and be dutiful towards him. As the husband has the responsibility to provide for his wife and protect her, she has the duty to be obedient to him within the limits set by Allaah. Many people often confuse this with meaning that the husband is allowed to abuse his wife or treat her as he wishes. This couldn't be further from the truth. Allaah says in the Holy Qur`an "... and live with them honourably". (4:19). In one Hadith, the Prophet [SAW] said "There is no obedience to anyone if it is disobedience to Allah. Verily, obedience is only in good conduct." Ṣaḥīḥ al-Bukhārī 6830, Ṣaḥīḥ Muslim 1840.

There are also examples in the Sunnah where the Prophet [S.A.W] would seek the advice of his wives and they would ask him questions. In fact, if your read about the relationship between the Prophet [SAW] and his wives, you will find that it certainly was not one of fear.

One of the most important tools needed to form a strong connection between the spouses is open and honest communication. Now, if a woman is forbidden to communicate openly to her husband because of culture, how then can she form a bond with him? If you want a beautiful marriage that is full of love and happiness, then you must allow your spouse to be free to express themselves fully without fear or apprehension.

Many of us will have been affected by negative cultural injustices between our parents that we may have witnessed in our households growing up. For many Muslims, the only example they know of a spousal relationship is their own parent`s marriage. Unfortunately, sometimes their parents' marriage may not have been the best example of a healthy marriage. We must be careful not to allow any oppressive cultural practices we may have witnessed growing up to affect our own marriages, consciously or subconsciously.

It may not always be easy for you to realise that you have been affected subconsciously by negative practices you have seen in your household growing up. Why? Because that is all you have ever known and you do not know any different. That is why we must emphasise the importance of being able to acknowledge our mistakes and being able to learn from our mistakes and grow. We must look to the Qur`an and authentic Hadeeth for guidance in all matters. We must realise that having a strong, positive marriage bond is not only for your own benefit, it will also shape the way that your children view marriage and set a standard for them to expect. If there ever was a negative cycle in your family, this is the time to break it - not just for your benefit, but also for the benefit of your children.

Another example of a negative cultural practice is the idea that the husband must not do any household chores. This is the opposite of the Sunnah of Prophet Muhammad [S.A.W] because we know that he used to help out at home in the household. In one Hadith, Al-Aswad reported: I asked Aisha, "What did the Prophet, peace, and blessings be upon him, do in his house?" Aisha said, "The Prophet would do chores for his family and he would go out when it was time for prayer." . Sahih al Bukhari 676.

To summarise, we must know when it is ok to take guidance from cultural traditions, and when to abandon them. As long as we remain in line with the teachings of the Qur`an and the Sunnah, we must abandon any cultural practices that oppress others.

Past Trauma

Past trauma refers to a negative event that happened in your childhood or early life that has influenced the way that you view the world, or the way you react to certain situations. Studies have shown that traumatic experiences can negatively impact individuals even decades after the event. Examples of common traumatic events can be child abuse, witnessing abuse, the death of a loved one, parents' divorce, or even relocation. There are many more examples and they can be different for each person. It is important to remember that we all cope with situations in different ways. So an event that you may have coped with well, could have been very traumatic for your spouse. You should take great care to never dismiss or downplay any event that your spouse tells you was traumatic or hurtful to them.

A traumatic event that happened in your childhood may have led you to view the world in a different way or to develop unhealthy habits as coping mechanisms. Coping mechanisms may include having a negative view of life, not wanting to socialise with others, problems trusting people, always expecting the worst, or running away from your problems.

Past trauma can make it difficult to bond with your spouse. for example, if somebody lost a loved one at a very young age, they may find it difficult to allow themselves to love people, because they are afraid of losing someone that they love again. In a marriage, the other spouse may view this as a case of their spouse not loving them and it could lead to a breakdown of the marriage. That is why it is so important to look back into your past and identify any traumas so that you are able to communicate them to your spouse. This way, they will be aware and will be able to understand you and your behaviours better. If you are the spouse feeling unloved, please do not keep quiet about it. Find a suitable time and speak to your partner about it in a loving manner.

It is important to discuss with your spouse the past experiences that may have caused them trauma so that you are best aware of how to support them. If you have been through a traumatic event it is advised to speak to your spouse about it and explain to them how it affected you and how it leads you to behave in certain ways. For example, you may have triggers from past experiences that your spouse should be aware of in order to avoid them.

Low Self-Esteem

Low self-esteem is a struggle that runs much deeper than beauty or outside appearance. People who suffer from low self-esteem often view themselves as not being worthy of love. They may feel as though they are not good enough for marriage and they may have a difficult time accepting that someone can truly love them and find them attractive. The feeling of having low self-esteem is a crippling sense of not being equal to other people because of the way that you look or because of what you believe to be true about yourself.

Low self-esteem can be developed through childhood experiences. Any experience that makes a child to constantly doubt themselves or to feel unloved can lead to an adult who has low self-esteem. Children crave attention and praise and it is for good reason. At that young age, children do not know who they are and so they rely on their authority figure to instill in them who they are and how they should feel about themselves. If you instill negative thoughts in their mind, that is what they will grow up believing. The way that we speak to our children today will become their inner voice as they grow up. So we must make a very conscious and consistent effort to praise our children and let them believe they are special and important and valued. Of course, this goes together with teaching them to be empathetic and respectful to others.

Examples of situations that can lead a child to develop low self-esteem are being constantly belittled and insulted by an adult or an authority figure. Studies have shown that some people may be more prone to low self-esteem than others. This would explain how siblings who have grown up in the same household can have different levels of self-esteem even though they would have been treated the same way by their authority figures.

Low self-esteem has a direct effect on a person's communication skills. One of the things that helps a solid marriage bond to be formed is being open and vulnerable with communication. Now a person who has low self-esteem may not be able to express their opinions and concerns because they do not view themselves as worthy of having an opinion. They may feel that their opinions do not matter. This person will also not want to be vulnerable because they are so fragile inside that they cannot risk being vulnerable. This can lead to the other spouse feeling that they are not opening up to them and this could begin to form a divide.

Low self-esteem is often associated with beauty and appearance.

If your spouse has low self-esteem, they may view themselves as unattractive and ugly. They may also not feel confident in their body. They will often be very self-critical of their appearance and you will find that they never accept a compliment. They may also find it difficult to be accepting and open during intimacy, leading to the frustration of the other spouse.

If you notice that your spouse has low self-esteem and it is affecting your marriage, it is important to not take it personally. Tell yourself that your spouse is behaving this way because of their own personal struggles. It is not because your spouse does not want to open up to you, rather, they are fighting a battle of their own inside. What you should do is to support them with encouraging words and compliments. Show them that they are loved and valued. Open up to them and be vulnerable and encourage them to do the same. With time, their self-esteem will begin to increase as they begin to feel safe in your love.

You could encourage your spouse to seek counselling or to open up to you about their low self-esteem issues. Often times when a problem is shared and someone feels understood, it is the beginning of healing. A great time to speak about such highly charged, emotional issues would be at night, in bed, with the lights switched off. There is something about being in the late hours of the night, with the cover and security of the darkness that encourages people to be more open with their feelings.

* * *

3. Islamic Bond

Research has shown that married couples who have a common interest are more likely to stay together. As a Muslim couple, you have Islam as a common interest and it can ` t get any better than that. With both of you being Muslims, you already know that your values and morals are similar. It is important that you and your spouse connect on a religious level because Islam is the way of life that you have both chosen and it is the biggest part of your identities. You should work on helping each other to get closer to Allaah. In this way, you will form a pure bond of loving each other for the sake of Allaah and you will achieve success in this world and in the hereafter. When you and your spouse make an effort to come closer to Allaah, your marriage will be filled with blessings from Allaah.

When a couple loves each other for the sake of Allah, it is a beautiful thing and it is the best type of love. Why? Because if your spouse loves you for the sake of Allaah, they will refrain from doing anything to harm you because they know that it will displease Allaah. Even if you have an argument with your spouse, they will still treat you well because they are aware that Allaah is watching. When your spouse is conscious of Allah, they will be motivated to treat you better - because they are aware that every little thing that they do for you they will be rewarded for it. They will be considerate of you because they will adhere to the Hadeeth that says "None of you will have faith until he loves for his brother what he loves for himself." Ṣaḥīḥ al-Bukhārī 13.

The Triangle

The relationship between the two spouses and Allaah can be shown in the analogy of a triangle. The closer that the spouses get to Allaah, the closer they will get to each other. I want you to have a look at the image of the triangle below. Can you see that as the husband and wife get closer to Allaah, they also get closer to each other automatically. Also notice that as the husband and wife get farther away from Allaah, the distance between them also increases. This simple example speaks volumes. The further away you are from Allaah, the further you will be from each other.

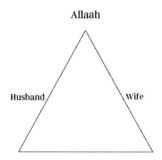

Worship Allaah Together

It is encouraged for a husband and wife to perform acts of worship together, and to encourage each other in performing good deeds.In the Holy Qur`an, Allaah praises the Prophet Zakariyah and his wife for their performing of good deeds. He says "Indeed, they used to hasten to good deeds and supplicate to Us in hope and fear, and they were to Us humbly submissive." 21:89.

Let me also draw your attention to the following Hadeeth. Abu Hurairah (R.A) reported: The Messenger of Allah [S.A.W] said, "May Allah show mercy to a man who gets up during the night and performs salat, awakens his wife to pray and if she refuses, he sprinkles water on her face (to make her get up). May Allah show mercy to a woman who gets up during the night and performs salat, awakens her husband for the same purpose; and if he refuses, she sprinkles water on his face." [Abu Dawud].This Hadeeth shows encouragement for the spouses to do worship together.

As a Muslim couple, you should be working toward having a good marriage here on earth, and also to be together in heaven. If you truly love each other, you should encourage each other to become better Muslims and better people each day. We are all on different levels of eman and that is ok. What Is important is that we try to better ourselves. Below are some things to do together as a couple to strengthen your Islamic bond. Remember that as you get closer to Allaah, your bond will increase automatically and Allaah will fill your home with love and blessings.

Pray together – Performing prayer is an act that we do to please Allaah but it also benefits us tremendously in our worldly life. People who pray are happier and more content. They show the ability to be reliable and committed which are needed qualities in a marriage. Remind your spouse of the importance of prayer and tell them you are reminding them because you want good for them. After the prayer, sit and reflect on Allaah and His power and grace. Encourage each other to pray and check up on each other. We know that success can only come from Allaah. So in order to have a successful marriage, we need to put Islam at the forefront of our married life.

Make dua together - Making dua is a very personal and private thing. When we make dua, we are at our most vulnerable as we ask Allaah to help us and fulfill our most inner needs and desires.

When you make dua with your spouse, you open up to each other and let each other into your vulnerable moments. Nothing builds a stronger bond than allowing yourself to be vulnerable to your spouse and trusting them to keep your vulnerability safe.

Read Qur`an together – Find some time often to read Quran with your spouse and contemplate on it. Translate it into a language that you can both understand and reflect on its powerful message. This is a beautiful practice that will become even more important when you have children. Allaah tells us that the Qur`an is a healer. It will heal our hearts from any unpleasant feelings such as jealousy, hatred, and anger. Allaah says in the Glorious Qur`an "We send down the Quran as a healing and mercy for the believers.." 17:82

Reading the Qur`an together is strongly encouraged especially when you are going through hardships in your marriage. It will help to bring tranquillity and healing to your hearts. It is also strongly encouraged to listen to the Qur`an recitation inside your house. Let your home be filled with the words of Allaah. This will create a positive household full of blessings from Allaah and it will help to expel the jinn who can certainly be mischief-makers.

Another activity you can do together is Qur`an memorisation. This is a great way to work towards a goal together. Allaah loves the deeds that are consistent even if they are small. So even if you memorise one Ayat a week together, this will please Allaah and increase blessings in your marriage. Choose a chapter that you both love and memorise it together.

Have deep conversations about Allaah, the Qur`an, and Islam. Perhaps you can contemplate the amazing scientific miracles of the Qur`an or perhaps you can choose one of Allaah`s names to reflect upon. You can reflect on the amazing stories of the Prophets before us and the righteous companions. It is recommended to have a religious activity that you do together each week.

Take turns to prepare a small sermon and read to each other. The sermon can be on anything Islamic and it certainly does not have to be lengthy. This is another beneficial activity to do especially when you have children. The point is to make Islam fit seamlessly into your daily married life.

Listen to Islamic lectures together – You can listen to Islamic lectures together to increase your knowledge of your deen. If you are going through a particular hardship, find a lecture about that topic and listen together then reflect.

Plan to make Hajj and Umrah together. This will give you a major goal to work towards and it will be the start of many conversations as you work together to achieve this goal. No doubt your bond will become stronger. It is important to have a religious goal to work towards because this keeps Islam at the forefront of your marriage.

Sponsor an orphan from a poor country and support them financially. - This will give you something to work on together, and it will be pleasing to Allaah. Other charitable things to do would include setting up a charity fund. It does not have to be something major. The two of you can have a sadaqah jar that you put money in at the end of every month. At the end of the year, you choose a cause to donate this money to. This may seem like a small deed but It is pleasing to Allaah and it is a project that you do together.

The truth is that in order for your marriage to flourish, you need Allaah`s blessings and mercy. There are many things we can recommend to help you form a beautiful marriage bond, but if the foundation of your marriage is not firm, then all could be in vain. It should come as no surprise to you that the foundation of your marriage should be to please Allaah.

It is important to connect on a religious level because you then have a higher power to be answerable to in regard to how you treat each other. Although it Is binding that you worship Allaah together, it is also important to remember not to overwhelm yourself. Allaah likes the deeds that are consistent even though they may be small. So make it a consistent routine to worship Allaah together. We are all on different levels of eman and so it is ok to start small, however, you must ensure that you are doing a religious act together. As Muslims we know that the ultimate success lies in the hereafter so It is important to help each other to build a good hereafter so that we can attain the ultimate success.

4. Communication

Communication is one of the most important building blocks that will determine the quality of a marriage. There is no doubt that the better the quality of your communication with your spouse, the better your marriage will be. To put it simply, good communication is a crucial factor in building a successful marriage.

So what exactly is communication? In its basic form, communication is the act of expressing yourself to another person. This can be in the form of speaking, writing, or body language. When it comes to Islamic marriage, communication plays an even more important role. This is because the spouses will not have spent much time together prior to marriage and will therefore need to quickly learn the best way to communicate effectively with each other. Learning the skills required for effective communication will help you to navigate this new normal called marriage.

Let's start by making it clear that communication in itself is pretty straightforward. As a matter of fact, we communicate many times throughout the day. However, effective communication is a skill that only a few have mastered. If you can master how to be an effective communicator, the quality of all the relationships in your life will improve drastically.

Set The Foundation

It is important to set the foundations for effective

communication in your marriage right from the very first time that you spend time together as a married couple. This will usually be on the night of your wedding. It is important to use this time to simply talk. Talk and get to know each other and ask all the questions that you need to - and then some more. Show your spouse that you are really interested in getting to know them.

Give your spouse your full attention. This means putting away your phone or any other distractions. One thing you must learn early on in your marriage is not to try and multitask when your spouse is speaking to you. Whenever possible, you must show your spouse that they have your full attention - especially during precious moments such as this.

On the night of your wedding, or the first time that you and your spouse spend time alone, it is normal that you will both be nervous and shy. So if your spouse seems quiet, uninterested, or even rude, do not hold it against them. Perhaps they may need more time to open up to you. What you must do is to be patient with them but you must keep talking. Do not make the mistake of being quiet because your spouse is also quiet. You must continue talking and to your surprise, they will begin to open up gradually. Remember that everyone has different characteristics. Some people are shyer than others and they may take a little longer to feel comfortable. Do not be discouraged if your spouse takes a while to open up. Have faith in the fact that you are both Muslims and therefore you have similar morals, values, and beliefs. That's a great starting point.

The Two Categories Of Communication

Communication can be split into two categories; daily communication and problem-solving communication. Daily communication is the communication that you do every day. This includes everything from giving salaam when you wake up in the morning to the text messages that you send each other throughout the day. It is important to have this communication at a good and comfortable level. If your daily communication is at a healthy level, it will make the second type of communication easier.

The second type of communication is problem-solving communication. This type of communication happens when you want to express your feelings to your spouse about an issue that affects you negatively. This is usually to let them know of something which they are doing that you do not like or maybe to confide in them about any other sensitive issue. You must be prepared for this type of communication because we cannot escape conflict in life. There will most definitely be a time when your spouse does something that annoys or displeases you. If you have a healthy level of daily communication in your marriage, it will be easier to initiate problem-solving communication when something does go wrong.

Communication is not something that is only done when a problem arises. Rather, you should have a good level of communication in your day-to-day lives. This will create an atmosphere that allows for easy expression of feelings when a problem does arise.

Did you know that lack of communication can also be a form of communication? That's right; if you do not speak to your partner they are going to be led into thinking that you are not interested in them. This is especially true at the beginning of the marriage before you get to know each other well. So even if you are a quiet individual or a man or woman of few words, you must make an effort to communicate with your spouse in a very expressive manner.

Constant Communication

As a married couple, it is important to communicate often and frequently. When you speak to each other often, you will begin to *know* each other and it will build a bond of friendship between the two of you. If your spouse is at work, send them a message and check on them. Do not wait for them to send you a message first. Ask them how their day is going and let them know that you are thinking about them. Do not undermine the importance of these small moments. It is certainly true that we all have busy lives, but you must prioritise your marriage. Even if you are short of time, you can make a five-minute call to your spouse and let them know you just wanted to hear their voice. This will make your spouse feel loved and valued. Make the phrases "I love you" and "I appreciate you" to be said often in your marriage.

We can never read the mind of another human being so you may have all these lovely thoughts inside your mind but it is only when you speak and express yourself that your spouse will be aware of them.

If you find yourself thinking about your spouse and how much you love and appreciate them, make it a point to send them a message and tell them straight away! Imagine how amazing it would feel if you received a random message from your spouse declaring their love and appreciation for you? It would be a great feeling. Oftentimes we love our spouses so much in our minds but we never fully express that love to them verbally. It's unfortunate because then your spouse never gets to realise the depth of your love for them. Remember that we can never read the minds of each other, so you may have all these lovely thoughts inside your mind but it is only when you express yourself that your spouse will be aware of them.

If your spouse spends the whole day at work or spends the whole day at home looking after the children, and there is no communication between the two of you - then something is seriously wrong. AlhamduliLaah, it is a great blessing that Allaah has blessed us with phones nowadays and He has made it easy for us to reach one another. Why not send your spouse a message from work asking how the day is? When you get a lunch break, take a few minutes to call your spouse and tell them that you just wanted to hear their voice. Your spouse will feel special that you are thinking of them. It does not have to be a serious conversation - it can be a simple one-line message or a 30-second phone call. If your spouse does not answer your call, why not leave them a funny or cheeky voice message? It is good to have an element of playfulness in your marriage.

Do you have that friend that you can spend hours on the phone with or that you call frequently when something happens? That is the way you should be with your spouse. Call your husband/ wife to tell them the silliest things or a joke that you just thought about. Marriage is more beautiful when you are husband and wife as well as best friends.

Compliments And Gratitude

Daily communication also includes complimenting your spouse and expressing gratitude. Complementing your spouse will make them feel loved and that you are attracted to them. This will lead to them having a confidence boost and a happy mood which will have a positive impact on both of you. Remember that compliments do not have to be about how a person looks, you can also compliment your spouse on their kind heart, on their parenting skills, and other characteristics that they possess.

Expressing gratitude is a really crucial thing in a marriage. When we get married, we essentially are there to make each other happy. It is important to express gratitude because it will make your spouse feel appreciated and seen for all they do for you. Often times you may find yourself thinking about your spouse and how much you love and appreciate them, you must make sure to actually express the words verbally or even in writing. Otherwise, it is just a thought that your spouse will never know.

Communicating with your spouse often will help you to understand your spouse and also to be understood. It is in these little daily moments of speaking that you will begin to *learn* who your spouse is and what are their likes and dislikes.

Effective Communication

Effective communication is not only about speaking, it is also about listening, understanding, contemplating, and showing empathy. When we communicate effectively, we allow ourselves to talk freely and openly without fear of judgment.

It is important for your spouse to feel that they can communicate with you freely. If your spouse does not feel safe expressing their feelings with you, then they will hold back from communicating with you. This will then result in your spouse going to find another person to talk to about your marital problems or they will keep everything inside and will not express their feelings to you. Over time this will build resentment and hatred will slowly begin to creep in.

An example of this is maybe your spouse is doing something that you do not like. It could be something that would have been easily solved had you spoken to your spouse directly and openly about it. However, because there is a lack of communication in your marriage, you do not address this issue with your spouse. Instead, you begin to imagine scenarios in your head as to why your spouse is doing this thing. You start to think that they must be doing it on purpose to hurt you. This will then lead to a whole scenario inside your mind and when you finally do talk about the issue, you will not talk, you will explode. Your spouse who may have been unaware of this problem the whole time will then react in a defensive manner and it will lead to an argument. All this could have been avoided had you communicated about the issue in an effective manner.

Consequences Of Ineffective Communication

It is important to note that when communication is not done effectively, it can actually cause more harm than good. Ineffective communication happens when you do not let your spouse know how truly deeply something affects you. An example is talking to your spouse about a problem that you have with them but not showing them the full extent of how it is really affecting you, instead, you downplay your feelings or even make a joke about it. Due to shyness or nervousness, you may play it off as a small issue. Now, your spouse may not take you seriously because you have not shown them the seriousness of the matter. They may then continue to do the habit and this will only make you angrier because you will think to yourself "but I already spoke to you about this! But you didn't change". Therefore, when you are communicating your feelings to your spouse, you must be very clear and direct in what you say.

Do not give hints or say things while you mean something else. You must communicate exactly as you feel and do so accurately. Remember, your spouse is not in your mind and the only way they can know your true feelings is if you verbalise them. Remember, this is the person that Allaah has chosen for you to spend the rest of your life with so be open to them.

Sometimes it may appear that your spouse is doing something purposely to hurt you. You may choose not to speak to him or her about it because you may think to yourself "this is so obvious! Of course he knows that I don't like it when he does that!". So you choose not to speak about it in the hopes that it will resolve on its own. This is not the right approach and it will build resentment. You must always communicate any issues to your spouse. Even if it is the case that your spouse is aware that they are doing something that you don't like, they may not realise just how much you hate it or how much it affects you. When you speak about it, they will then realise the effects of their actions and stop.

We have to remember that shaytan is an open enemy to us and he tries to sow discord between us. There is nothing he loves more than when you start to have bad thoughts about your spouse and he will do all he can to accelerate those bad thoughts. When you feel yourself starting to get frustrated, seek refuge in Allaah from the shaytan and ask Allaah to show you a better way.

One mistake that is often made by couples is that we expect the other person to be a mind reader. We expect the other person to know what we want and what we expect from them. This is a really dangerous game because your spouse will never know what is in your mind so they will always fall short. Whatever the situation is, break it down to them and be clear on how it makes you feel. Remember that we all grew up in different households, different cultures, and had different experiences which shaped us and our outlooks on life. Something which may seem so obvious to you may not be obvious to the other person. You may have been able to get away with not communicating effectively with your siblings or parents, but the dynamic in a marriage is completely different. It is one that can only survive when both spouses are willing to be open, honest, and considerate.

Communication Etiquette

It is important that when we want to communicate to our spouse, we do so in a polite and respectful manner and use words that are clear and cannot be interpreted as being rude or disrespectful. Often times you may be right but the way in which you present your point can make it difficult for your spouse to accept what you are saying. As the saying goes, delivery is everything.

The importance of communicating in a good manner is actually mentioned in a beautiful Ayat in the Holy Qur'an when Allaah says "Tell my worshipers to say always that which is best: truly,

Satan is always ready to stir trouble among them - Satan is clearly man's enemy." 17:53. This Ayat shows us that shaytan is always ready to plant seeds of enmity amongst us using our own words so we must be careful to structure our words in the best way possible.

Sometimes in your marriage, you may find it difficult to communicate with your spouse. You may feel embarrassed or you may think that your spouse will judge you or think of you a certain way. It is important to push these thoughts to the back of your mind and express your feelings openly and clearly. why? Because your spouse is the closest person to you, both physically and emotionally and you should feel free to speak about any issue that makes you uncomfortable or perturbed. In many cultures, women are encouraged to not speak up to their husbands and to deal in silence with any pain that he may cause her. This is not from Islam and we must abandon these archaic practices which are oppressive. Do not think of any issue as insignificant. It is these insignificant issues that will pile up and form a colossal problem.

Communicate clearly and do not leave any room for misinterpretation. It could be that your spouse was completely unaware of the problem that you are facing. Even if your spouse was aware of the problem, when you address it and talk about it in a clear and direct manner, you allow your spouse the responsibility to fulfill what you have asked of them. You allow them a chance to reassure you and commit to doing better. By the end of the conversation, you will have a stronger bond as you will feel understood.

We must be aware that communication is a two-way exchange. So as much as we put emphasis on the person expressing themselves to do so effectively, we must also emphasise the importance of the listener to be attentive and respectful. When your spouse communicates to you something which they dislike from you, you must listen attentively and show them that you value their opinion. Remember, this is a vulnerable moment for them and if they sense even the slightest disregard from you, they will immediately close up and that will put a block to any further communication. And do you know what's worse? next time, they will not bother to express their feelings to you.

When your spouse is telling you about something meaningful to them, stop what you are doing and face them directly. Show them that they are important and you want to listen to what they are saying. This simple act of putting your phone down and looking at them or turning away from the kitchen and facing them will have a really big positive impact. Straight away your spouse will feel supported. You could ask questions to show that you are interested and concerned. You can even rephrase what they said to you in order to show them that you understood them well. Statements of validation such as " that must have been hard for you to deal with" or "what can I do better to support you" - go a long way to show that you care and value your spouse, and their feelings are important to you.

A large part of being a good communicator is being a good listener. You must learn the skill of making your spouse feel that you have understood what they have said and that it is of utmost importance to you. This will make your spouse feel valued, validated, and understood. And there is no better feeling than to be understood and validated. We know from the character of our beloved Prophet ﷺ that when he spoke to someone, he would turn his full body around and completely face the person. This shows that he gave his full attention to the person he was speaking to. This makes the person speaking to feel like they are important and that you value what they have to say.

Show your spouse that you are interested in what they are saying by looking at them when they are speaking to you. Don't be shy to make eye contact and look your spouse directly in the eye. This is your husband/wife that Allaah has chosen for you. Studies show us that looking at each other in the eye increases empathy, so If your spouse is talking about something that is upsetting, turn to them and hold their hand gently. Give their hand a squeeze to reassure them that you are there and you are listening and you understand.

Sometimes you may not know the right things to say and that is ok. In this case, look at your spouse and let them know that you may not know the right words to say to comfort them but you are there for them.

If your spouse is speaking to you about an issue that they have with something that you are doing, you should start by acknowledging their feelings. Let them know that you were not aware that they felt this way or that your actions were being interpreted in this way. You should work out a way with your spouse to solve this issue. Ask your spouse for their input on how you can make things better. For example, you could say "How can I improve on that?" or " I would never want to hurt you, so tell me how I can fix this." This will make them feel valued and important to you. Statements such as this may be hard to say. Perhaps you may want to say them but you feel somewhat shy or vulnerable. This is normal, but you must fight that feeling and push through. Remember this is the one person in the world that you can fully open up to. Take small steps and you will be surprised at how Allaah will make it easy for you. It is important to let go of any pride and ego and be ready to change to become a better person for your spouse.

It is important to emphasise again that you should never assume that your spouse knows what they are doing wrong. Remember, even if your spouse does know what they are doing wrong and they choose to continue doing it, it is still important to talk about it because you then hold them accountable and they now have the responsibility to stop it. But if you keep quiet, they can carry on without any accountability. You should find a time when your spouse is relaxed to bring up the conversation. You should express clearly exactly what it is that is bothering you. Many times, we tend to hide our true feelings or give hints instead of saying exactly what we want. You have to remember that this is your partner and this marriage is forever so do not be afraid to say exactly what is making you unhappy.

Nobody likes to be told that they are doing things wrong. It tends to be more prominent in men to have an ego and not want to be told of any flaws they may have - especially coming from their wife. This is rooted in cultural ignorance and it has no place in Islam. This is because a Muslim must always be willing to better themselves and they must be self-critical in order to avoid hurting the feelings of another Muslim.

It is completely understandable that communicating your feelings to your spouse may be hard in the early days. This could be due to shyness or not wanting to do anything that may upset your spouse. What can be done is that you can write your feelings in a letter to your spouse and let them read it while you are there. That way it will be easier to express what you truly mean. Remember that healthy, successful marriages include uncomfortable conversations.

Many of us may have inherited toxic communication traits from our childhood through watching our own parents' marriages. It could be the case of the father shouting at the mother or the mother ignoring him with the silent treatment. Or maybe you witnessed your mother being afraid to speak to your father about an issue that was bothering her. As children, we pick up on these behaviours and subconsciously they begin to take effect on our own marriages. We have to take time to sit and evaluate ourselves to figure out any childhood trauma that we may have experienced growing up and ask ourselves if this has affected our marriages. It is only when we can acknowledge the trauma that we are able to overcome it.

Let me let you in on a little secret! Communication is not always fun! It's not always easy and you probably will feel uncomfortable doing it. Remember that it is normal to feel a little apprehensive because when you communicate effectively, you are being vulnerable. Being vulnerable and expressing your inner feelings is difficult because it leaves you open to being hurt if those feelings are not respected or reciprocated. So the next time that you feel awkward and a bit shy when communicating, it's because you're doing it right and I promise it will get easier over time.

If you find that communicating your feelings is unbearably difficult, then it may be linked to having low self-esteem. This is an issue discussed in earlier chapters of this book.

* * *

5. Expectations

One of the most important things to communicate clearly to your spouse are your expectations of marriage. This should be a conversation that you have in the early days of your marriage. You must remember that you and your spouse are two different people who grew up in completely different households. You will have different expectations of marriage. Your spouse will not be able to read your mind. The only way that they will know what you expect from them is if you tell them directly.

What are the things that you would expect from your husband or wife? What do you expect from marriage? What are your boundaries? It is essential to make this clear to your spouse. Expectations are important because when your expectations are met, you will be happy in your marriage and feel respected, valued and satisfied.

We will all have different expectations of marriage. These expectations will be based on our own experiences growing up. For example, what we saw from our parents or even what we watched on television. Some expectations are major and will need to be discussed even before the marriage, for example, a man may expect his wife to stay home and not work once they are married. Or he may expect his wife to live with his parents. Other expectations are smaller but still important and valid. Such as expecting your husband to be romantic towards you and buy you flowers, or expecting your husband to help you with household chores when he is available.

It may be difficult to express all your expectations at the

beginning of your marriage due to shyness. However, as the marriage progresses, be sure to let your spouse know exactly what you would expect from them. When we do not let our spouses know what our expectations are, how then can we be angry with them when they do not meet these expectations?

Types Of Expectations

Expectations can be about finances, intimacy, childbearing and raising, household chores, and many others. Each marriage is as unique as the two people within it.

Expectations about the running of your household are particularly important. Distribute the duties amongst yourselves so that everyone is aware of their responsibilities and nobody is feeling overworked. It is the traditional way that the husband works while the wife looks after the house and the children. However, each family is different and you must reach an agreement that works best for your household.

In most families, it will be the role of the wife to look after the home while the husband goes out to work. The wife must take this responsibility very seriously and do her best to accomplish it well. As a wife, you should feel proud and happy to look after your home and to please your husband. It is within the nature of a woman to want to nurture and look after her home, her husband, and her children. This is a duty that you must accomplish, in the same way that your husband has to go to work and that is his duty that he must fulfil.

It is important for the wife to create a comfortable home for herself, her husband, and her children. This includes making sure that the husband comes home to a clean and tidy home, with a meal ready for him. This will go a long way in creating a strong bond between the two of you because he will notice the effort that you are making for him. Doing this for your husband will not only show him love, but it will also show him care and respect. He will always look forward to coming home because he knows that he will find peace and rest.

In many homes, the wife will also go to work, and therefore the husband cannot expect his wife to work a full time job and still be able to maintain the household on her own. He must remember that she is only a human being like himself and he must help her out and share the duties in a fair manner.

The duties of looking after the home can quickly become overwhelming - especially after a woman has children or if she works outside the home. The husband must therefore be considerate of his wife and help her. When each spouse pays attention to ensure that they fulfill their duty to the other, then the marriage will run smoothly and you will both be happy.

Expectations about intimacy are likely to be different between wife and husband because of the way that Allaah created men and women to be different. It Is important to communicate to each other your needs and desires around the subject of intimacy. This is definitely something that may be awkward to speak about at the beginning of your marriage, but as time goes on, you must learn to open up to each other.

Expectations around intimacy may be based on issues such as how often you are intimate and what you each expect from intimacy. The subject of intimacy is often overlooked by women, yet it is very important to men. Make no mistake that it is a very important issue and failure to get this right will damage your marriage greatly. A Hadeeth which highlights the importance of this issue was narrated by Talq ibn Ali who reported that the Messenger of Allah [SAW] said, "If a man calls his wife to fulfil his needs, let her come to him even if she is over the oven." Sunan al-Tirmidhī 1160.

If your spouse's expectations for intimacy are met, they will be happy and this will have a direct positive effect on the whole marriage.

Finances are something that is often left unspoken about in marriage until it is too late. It is almost seen as taboo to discuss finances. As a couple, you should discuss your finances openly and make plans for how to run your household. For example, you should know the budget of the household and be clear on it so that one spouse doesn't overspend and the other spouse is not seen as stingy. Statistics show that financial problems are the second leading cause of divorce. Of course, finances can go up and down in life and priorities can change so that you may have less or more money to spend. The key to navigating any issues is to make sure that you are communicating well with each other.

Expectations in a marriage do not always have to be major. Sometimes the small expectations are more important because they are the ones that make up our daily lives. Let your spouse know the simple things you expect for them. For example, this could be to do the grocery shopping together, or that you spend some time together once a week. Or maybe you expect romantic gestures from your spouse. These are all valid needs and so don't be shy to express them.

It is important to note that there may be times when you have to lower your expectations and make compromises in your marriage.

* * *

6. Build Friendship

Marriage should be a place of laughter and happiness. Humour has a funny way of bonding people together. When someone makes you laugh, you want to be around them all the time. Your spouse should be your best friend, they should be the person that you want to hang out with all the time and the one that you can stay up with talking for hours at night.

Unfortunately, in some cultures, women are taught to be afraid of their husbands. They are told never to answer back, and if ever their husband should wrong them, they must bear it with patience. This is not right, and it is unjust. Do not be fooled by culture because there is no place in Islam where a husband is allowed to be unjust to his wife or to abuse her In any way. In fact, it is quite the opposite. Allaah tells us in the Glorious Qur`an "… and live with them honourably". (4:19). This tells us that the husband must treat his wife with honor. What is the definition of honour? It is to have a high level of respect, to hold them in high esteem – almost as if it is a privilege to be with them.

As a husband, it is your duty to make sure that your wife feels comfortable with you. That she feels safe from physical harm, as well as emotional harm. Do not speak to her words that are hurtful, nor should you raise your voice to her. How sad is the situation of a marriage where the wife is constantly on edge about the wrath of her husband should she displease him. Abdullah bin Amr reported that the Prophet [SAW] said: The Muslim is the one from whose tongue and hand the Muslims are safe. Ṣaḥīḥ al-Bukhārī 10.

I will quote a Hadith from the Prophet [SAW] to further emphasise this fact. Abu Huraira reported that the Messenger of Allah [SAW] said, "The most complete of believers in faith are those with the best character, and the best of you are the best in behavior to their women." It is unfortunate that many husbands will show their best face to their friends and not to their wife.

It must be noted that the same advice applies to women towards their husbands. They must also be kind and speak good words. However, greater emphasis has been put on the husband here because statistics show that women are more at risk of being abused. This is especially true when culture comes into play. Remember that the hurtful words may roll off your tongue easily, but once they are said, they can never be taken back. Constantly abusing your spouse will cause resentment to begin to grow in their heart towards you, even though they may not show this.

Friendship

You can form a friendship with your spouse by spending time together with them and doing fun things together. Discover the things that you have in common with your spouse and bond on those things. It can be on Islam, a love of food, animals, a passion you both have, or anything else. The more things you have in common, the closer your bond will be.

Another great way of building a friendship with your spouse is showing interest in what they love. We all have our hobbies and things we are interested in. If you know your spouse loves a particular sport or has a hobby, take some time to learn about It so that you can talk about it and maybe arrange to do a fun activity. Your spouse will certainly appreciate your interest.

Have fun with your spouse! We know that the Prophet [S.A.W] went racing with his wife Aisha [R.A] in a playful manner. Aisha said, "I raced him on foot and I outran him, but when I gained some weight, I raced him again and he outran me. The Prophet said: This is for that race." [Sunan Abī Dāwūd 2578] This shows us an example of being playful with your spouse and having fun. Over time you will have your own private jokes which is a small step on the road to creating your own unique bond.

It was also said by Ibn Kathir that "It was the character of the Prophet to live in a beautiful manner with his wives, being cheerful and kind to them, generously spending on them, and laughing with them." Source: Tafsīr Ibn Kathīr 4:19.

The essence of friendship is to be able to be yourself around someone without fear of judgment. So work towards being fully comfortable around your spouse and being yourself. This may take some time especially for newly wedded couples, but it will make the marriage fun and relaxed. Marriage in Islam is supposed to be a safe place for both couples to love each other and be comfortable in every way. Do not try to be too structured in how you speak to your spouse. Be free and be yourself. This marriage is to last a lifetime so it is important to be yourself.

❋ ❋ ❋

7. Love Languages

Love language is a term used to describe the way in which a person shows love and recognises love. The term love language is derived from the best-selling book by Dr. Gary Chapman called "the five love languages. The secret to love that lasts"

Did you know that we all show love in different ways? And that we also recognise love in different ways? The way that one person shows love may be completely different from another person. You may do an act of love for your spouse but they may not recognise it as such because their love language may be different from yours.

It is not necessary to have the same love language as your spouse in order for a marriage to work. Of Course, that would make things a lot easier when it comes to understanding each other. However, it is possible for a marriage to succeed and thrive even if the spouses have two completely different love languages. It may require a little more effort but it is very easy to learn the love language of your spouse so that you know how to show them love in a way that they can recognise, appreciate, and reciprocate.

Understanding love languages is extremely important in marriage because it will help you to understand how your spouse shows love to you and how they like to be shown love. It is important to understand how your spouse likes to be shown love so that you are able to give them love in a way that they can recognise it. If you do not show your partner love in a way that they recognise, it may result in them feeling unloved.

Love languages are even more important when it comes to marriage in Islam. This is because most couples will discover each other's love languages during the "dating phase". However, we do not have a "dating phase " in Islam. So we have to find out the love language of our spouse once we are in the marriage. Hence why it is important to be educated on love languages so that you can be aware of what to look out for and start to implement them right away.

You can think of love languages as a shortcut to finding out how to love your spouse. Once you have a good understanding of what love languages are, making your spouse feel loved will be effortless, effective, and enjoyable!

Types Of Love Languages

According to Dr. Chapman, love languages can be divided into five categories. Most people will have one primary love language that they identify with the most. Below are the five love languages explained with examples.

1. Words of affirmation
2. Physical touch
3. Quality time
4. Giving gifts
5. Acts of service

Words Of Affirmation

This love language is all about the power of words, acknowledgment, and affirmation. As human beings, we are all affected by words but some of us are more sensitive to them than others. If your love language is words of affirmation, then you feel deeply loved and valued when your spouse verbally expresses their love to you. This also includes written notes or text messages expressing their love for you.

Do you like to hear your partner clearly tell you "I love you"? Do you notice if a day goes by without your spouse telling you that they love you? Do you always make sure to end a phone call with the words "love you"? If that sounds like you, then your love language could be "words of affirmation." You like to be told clearly that you are loved and to be reassured often in your relationship. You also like to reassure those whom you love that you love them - constantly.

A beautiful example of how this love language played out in the life of the Prophet ﷺ is shown in the tale that is narrated that Aisha (may Allaah be pleased with her) asked the Prophet [S.A.W] : "How is your love for me?" The Prophet [S.A.W] replied, "Like the rope's knot". (to signify that the love was secure and strong) every so often after that, she would ask him, "How is the knot?" and he would reply "The same as ever". (reported in Hiya al Awliya). This is a beautiful example of the Prophet [S.A.W] affirming his love for his wife and making her feel secure in her marriage with him. Once a woman feels secure in her marriage, she is truly able to open up her heart to love you and this will create such a special and unique marital bond. Do not assume that your spouse knows that you love them - you must express it verbally.

It is important not to mistake this love language with being "needy". No, rather it is simply that we are all created differently and our brains process emotions differently. A Hadeeth comes to mind where our beloved Prophet [S.A.W] said "If one of you loves his brother for the sake of Allaah, let him tell him, for it does good and makes the love last." [Shaykh al-Albaani said it is mursal with a saheeh isnaad.]

The Hadeeth above, and others similar to it, show us the importance of expressing love verbally. And we are guaranteed by our Prophet [S.A.W] that this will increase love between us. The Prophet [S.A.W] recommended us to express clearly our love for our fellow brothers and sisters - so what about in the case of a husband and wife! It must be more important and crucial to do so.

Tips On Implementing "Words Of Affirmation"

Make a conscious effort to tell your partner clearly that you love them every day.

Make sure your partner feels confident and assured in your love. You could try saying phrases like "I am happy to be with you" or "AlhamduliLaah you are the person I have been looking for all my life"

Write a letter to your spouse stating all the reasons you love them and post it. Imagine the look on their face when they open it and read the beautiful words. They will feel special and loved.

Leave little surprise notes for your spouse telling them how much you love and appreciate them.

Physical Touch

Do you like to hold hands with your spouse when you are on an outing or even when you are at home? When your spouse does something nice for you, do you always have to thank them with a hug? If those sound like you, then your love language could be "physical touch." This means that You feel loved when you physically connect with someone either through hugging, kissing, or physical intimacy.

Often it is assumed that this love language is only for men but this is not true. It is also the primary love language for many women. People who have physical touch as their love language feel a deep connection with their spouse through physical gestures. Intimacy is very important to them as they may feel most connected to you at that time. It is therefore important that you make the extra effort to make them feel loved during intimacy.

Tips on implementing "physical touch"

When your partner returns from work, greet them with a long hug

Offer frequent, spontaneous massages to your spouse.

Hold hands with your spouse, even at home.

Plan ahead for intimacy and show your partner that you made extra effort to make intimacy a special time.

Quality Time

People who have "quality time" as their love language feel most connected to their spouse when it is just the two of them and they have undivided attention. Do you look foward to the moment your husband will get home from work so that you can sit and tell him all about your day? Would you rather spend the night talking with your wife into the late hours, Just the two of you? Do you look forward to date nights with your husband when it's just the two of you? In that case, your love language may be quality time. You value so much the moments you spend with just you and your spouse when you have their undivided attention. When your spouse makes time for you, you feel that they love you.

This is another love language that may come off as being "needy". However, once you understand your spouse, you will realise that this is not the case at all. This person values a deeper connection. Time is the most valuable thing we have and this spouse wants to share that with you.

Tips On Implementing "Quality Time"

Plan a date night every week with your partner and stick to the schedule.

Book a road trip where you drive for long hours and just talk

Plan some quiet time maybe once a week where you sit and read Quran together

Try and have some time at the end of each day to just sit and talk with your partner

Receiving Gifts

Do you believe in the saying "it's the thought that counts"? Do you feel loved and special when someone gives you a gift? If so, then receiving gifts could be your primary love language. You really appreciate the time and the effort that your spouse puts in to find you a gift that will make you happy. You feel loved because he/she was thinking about you and went out of their way to buy you something to make you happy. This is not necessarily about spending money on an expensive gift, it is more about the fact that you thought about your spouse and did this to make them happy.

A very well-known Hadeeth comes to mind when we speak about this love language. The Prophet [S.A.W] said: "Exchange gifts, as that will lead to increasing your love to one another." [Al-Bukhari]. In this Hadeeth, we have another guaranteed way of increasing love between each other. Often it is left to the husband to be the one who always buys gifts for his wife. While this is great, It is also important for the wife to gift her husband. We must remember that men are also in need of love.

If you find out that the love language of your spouse is receiving gifts, then it is time to start listening and taking notes! What does he talk about all the time? What is that handbag that she has been talking about getting for months? What is his favourite perfume? Does she love flowers? Make mental notes so that you can surprise your spouse with gifts.

Tips On Implementing "Receiving Gifts"

Buy your partner flowers often.

Come home with his/her favourite chocolate or snack.

Buy your spouse something and say " when I saw this I just thought of you straight away"

Acts Of Service

If "acts of service" is your love language, then you feel loved when your partner takes care of something that you were supposed to do. You really appreciate that they did something for you, just so that they can make your life easier. For example, if they do the washing up for you or they run to the post office to drop off your parcels. You really appreciate your partner giving up their time to take care of one of your tasks. If you can relate to that, then your love language may be acts of service. The acts of service do not have to be big and tiresome. A simple helping hand is greatly appreciated.

Tips On Implementing "Acts Of Service"

Wake up early one day and make your spouse breakfast in bed

Make a packed lunch for your husband to take to work

Offer to do the kids` bedtime routine whilst your wife has a cup of tea

Take care of a task that your spouse was supposed to be in charge of

Figure Out Your Love Language

The first step to understanding love languages is to figure out your own love language. It can certainly be difficult to figure out your love language because love comes in a variety of forms and you may feel that you cannot pinpoint a single one. For example, you may love to spend quality time with your spouse, but you also love to receive gifts. However, most people will find that they have one primary love language that most relates to them.

The easiest way to find out your love language is to take a quiz that was invented by the author of the book. This quiz involves answering a set of questions and then you will be matched to the love language that best matched your responses. Another way to figure out your love language is to think about how you show love. The way that you show love will also be the way that you like to receive it. For example, if you are a person that loves to give gifts to those that you love, then it is likely that your love language is receiving gifts.

Once you have your love language figured out, you should inform your spouse what it is and tell them examples of how you relate to this love language.

How To Find Out The Love Language Of Your Spouse

Once you have figured out your love language, it is now time to figure out the love language of your spouse. It is incumbent upon you to understand the love language of your spouse.

We often see situations where one spouse feels unloved by their partner when actually, it was just a case of not understanding each other. It could be that your spouse does love you, but they show love in a different way, For example; a wife may say "he doesnt love me, he never tells me that he loves me" and the husband will reply "what? what do you mean I dont love you? I just bought for you a new handbag the other day!" can you see how their love languages are conflicting there? Clearly, her love language is words of affirmation and his love language is receiving gifts. But because they have not communicated this to each other, it has led to conflict in the marriage. The husband thinks that giving her gifts is enough to make her feel loved, but her love language is words of affirmation, so she needs to hear him verbalise his love to her. This is an example of why it is so crucial to learn each other's love languages and use them to show love.

There is only one way to find out your partner's love language and that is through communication. Simply ask your husband or wife - what do I do that makes you feel loved? Or what can I do for you to show you that I love you? You could also ask your partner to take an online quiz to find out their love language.

A great activity to do together on the wedding night or on a date is to do a quiz together to determine each other's love language. It can be a fun ice breaker and it will get you talking and opening up to each other. Also, it will give you a starting point to knowing what your spouse likes.

Love Languages Can Change

Love languages may change as time passes and your relationship grows into different stages. For example, after having children, a woman's love language may change and she may begin to value more the acts of service you do to assist her as she now has less free time because of the baby. If the love language of your husband is quality time, then this will be affected greatly when a child is born as you will not have as much time available to spend together. It is important to have frequent discussions with each other so you can always know how to best stay connected with each other.

* * *

8. Romance And Affection

R omance and affection are the two things that distinguish your spouse from being just a friend to being a husband or a wife. In a marriage where there is no romance and affection, then you are just two friends living together, you are not actually a married couple. In the Muslim community, speaking about romance appears to be a taboo subject. Many people will shy away from this topic - not because it is unimportant, but because they are simply too embarrassed to speak about it. Whilst I can appreciate that many of these taboos may originate from culture, it is not a good enough excuse and we must talk about this important topic. Why? Because women nowadays are no longer prepared to stay in marriages where there is no love and romance.

Muslim women at the time of marriage are often told that love is not something that is important in a marriage. Instead, they are reminded of the duties and responsibilities that they must do for their husbands. No emphasis is put on the importance of the husband to show love and be romantic. In the same way, men are not told the importance of romance in marriage and so they do not see it as something that they have to do.

In many cases, even though a girl may not have been told directly that romance is not important in marriage, she will have picked up that notion by never witnessing her parents showing any romance or affection between each other. In a similar way, many husbands may find it strange to show affection to their wives because they never witnessed this between their parents. There are different levels of romance and there is a type that can be shown in front of children. For example, the husband buys his wife flowers, or praises her, or sits next to her.

Romance is a very important aspect of marriage and it must be treated as such. The Muslim husband must realise that being romantic and affectionate to his wife is a duty that he must fulfil. Both spouses must prioritise being romantic to each other. Do not view romance as a luxury in marriage, no, rather it is a necessity.

It Is in the nature of a woman to want to be chased and wooed by her husband, just like it is in the nature of a man to want to chase the female and impress her. Many Muslim men feel that once the nikah has been done and they have paid the mahr, they no longer need to work for their wife's love by being romantic. This is very detrimental to our marriages. It leaves the woman feeling unloved and as though marriage is a chore.

Romance and affection can be described as the way a couple shows love to each other. We have a great example to follow in the Prophet Muhammad [S.A.W]. Let me give you an example of how he encouraged us to openly show affection. On one occasion, the Prophet Muhammad [S.A.W] was asked by one of his companions – "Which person is most beloved to you?" Without hesitation, he replied "Aisha". (Sahih Bukahri 3462 ,Sahih Muslim 2384). Look at how the Prophet [S.A.W] was quick to let the people know that he loved his wife. He was not ashamed nor was he embarrassed. Many men would struggle to express their love to their wives directly, let alone in the presence of other men.

When speaking about romance, it is important to note that men also need to be shown love and romance. The advice given is to both husbands and wives. However, it is notable that the duty to be romantic falls more on the husband than on the wife. This is particularly true at the beginning of the marriage before you are accustomed to each other. This is simply due to the dynamic that Allaah has created between the spouses.

Saying "I Love You"

Romance and affection are lacking greatly in many marriages, to the extent that even a couple that have been married for many years may struggle to look each other in the eye and say the words "I love you". In fact, It is sometimes seen as weak for a man to express his love to his wife.

It is understandable that sometimes you may feel shy and hesitant to express your love to your spouse. This is understandable because it is something completely new. It would help to remember that the Prophet [S.A.W] encouraged us to spread love amongst each other verbally and directly. Al-Miqdam ibn Ma'dikarib reported: The Messenger of Allah [S.A.W] said, "When one of you loves his brother, let him know." (Sunan al-Tirmidhī 2392).

So when you feel shy to express your love, remember this Hadeeth and remember that when you express your love to your spouse you actually get rewarded for it. Some people may argue that they show love to their spouse in other ways and they do not have to say directly "I love you". I would strongly disagree with this notion.

No matter what else you are doing to show your love, you should also be saying it directly to your spouse. There is no escaping it! The Hadith above shows us that it is important to express your love verbally and directly. Remember that the Prophet ﷺ did not speak of his own desire but rather he was inspired by Allaah. Allaah knows our hearts and He knows what we need. Will it be a little awkward the first time that you say "I love you" to your spouse? most definitely, but I promise it will get easier and it will become like second nature.

If you come from a culture where you never really heard your parents say the words "I love you" to each other, then it may be difficult for you to implement this in your own marriage. That is understandable, but you must remember that in order to have a strong marriage bond, you have to put in work and effort and you have to be prepared to make changes. It may be uncomfortable at times, but it will be worth it in the end. Wouldn't you love to be able to express your love to your spouse and children freely?

According to the author of the book we have discussed called "love languages", the most popular love language is `words of affirmation`. In other words, most people recognise love when it is said to them directly. So if you neglect to tell your spouse directly that you love them, it could leave them feeling unloved, regardless of what else you are doing for them.

When you tell your spouse that you love them, you make them feel special, accepted, and wanted. If you find it difficult to say the words directly, maybe you can start by writing them in a text message or even on a note and leave it to surprise your spouse. It is these small and thoughtful gestures that will really turn your spouse's heart towards you.

Once you are comfortable expressing your love to your spouse, why not take it a step further and tell them why you love them. Tell them what you love about them and be vulnerable and open up to your spouse. Expressing love so deeply and openly can leave you feeling vulnerable and it is a brave thing to do. When you are vulnerable and open to your spouse, they can immediately sense it and it encourages them to do the same.

The words "I love you" should be a common phrase in your marriage. Allow those words to flow out of your mouth often and easily. If you are newly married, make it a common practice to say the words "I love you" often. If you have been married for a while, it is not too late to start to implement this. Start today and I promise you, your spouse will also start saying it too. Yes, it may be awkward and even uncomfortable the first few times but you must push through and continue. Remember that you are strengthening your marriage bond and also getting rewards from Allaah too.

Be Romantic!

You must make a conscious effort to be romantic to your spouse. Many Muslim couples will not make any effort to be romantic and they somehow expect love and romance to appear. Unfortunately, it does not work like that. Romance must be carefully planned in a marriage. Please do not expect it to be like the movies where people fall in love at first sight and they live happily ever after. No, you have to put effort into the marriage to form a bond and fall in love. Falling in love is something that can perhaps happen easily, however, staying in love is a conscious decision that you must make every day.

At the beginning of a marriage, between excitement and nervousness, lust can easily be confused for love. As the honeymoon phase passes, the couple then begins to realise that their love is dwindling away. Love, just like everything else in this world, will begin to decrease if it is not maintained well. You can make sure that you stay in love with your spouse by putting in targeted effort to do romantic and affectionate things for your spouse.

Have you heard people speak of the feeling of having "butterflies in my tummy". This is a term people use to describe the feeling of love and excitement they have for their spouse. It is possible to achieve this feeling and have that spark in your marriage. The way to do so is by making a conscious effort to maintain romance and affection in your marriage.

Types Of Romance

Romance can be roughly divided into two types. The first type is daily romance, and the second type is special romance. Daily romances are the little affectionate things that we do for our spouses each day. In some instances, you may not even realise that these actions are affectionate. You should make these actions so prominent in your marriage that they become second nature and you do them even without thinking. Examples of daily romances are holding hands or embracing.

Special romances are the bigger displays of affection that we do for our spouses. These can be done less frequently and they may cost more money and time. Examples of these can be buying your spouse flowers, going on a date, or even going on a trip away together. You may be surprised to learn that daily romances are more important and will have a greater positive impact on your marriage than special romances. Do not wait to be romantic to your spouse only after you've had an argument or only on special occasions like Eid.

The essence of romance is doing nice things for each other. Put simply, it comes down to taking the effort to do things that will make your spouse happy. Show your spouse that you care about them so much that you are prepared to put their needs above your own. This could be by doing something as simple as letting your wife sleep in and you wake up early and take care of the children. Marriage is all about sacrificing little and big things for the pleasure of your spouse. Below are some examples of ways in which you can show romance and affection.

Examples Of Romance And Affection

Holding hands – Holding hands with your spouse is highly underrated. Studies have shown that holding hands with your spouse causes the brain to release a chemical called oxytocin. This is a powerful chemical released in the brain which has been nicknamed `the bonding hormone` due to its role in forming emotional connections. Holding hands provides a sense of safety and security and this is particularly important for women as they like to feel safe and protected. It makes you and your spouse feel so connected as if you are one person. Couples in thriving marriages may find they automatically hold hands even without realising it.

Holding hands does not have to be done in public. In fact, it Is encouraged to hold your spouse's hand at home.

When your spouse is upset or is telling you something that was perhaps upsetting or traumatic, you should hold their hand firmly to reassure them and let them know that you are there for them. When you hold your spouse's hand, you should interlock your fingers together so that your palms are touching. It is interesting to note that your palms have pressure points which when pressed firmly, will trigger the brain to release a chemical known as cortisol. Cortisol is the stress relief hormone. So when your hold the hand of your spouse firmly, it will make them feel relaxed and so close and connected to you. Perhaps when your spouse returns home from a long day, give their hand a gentle massage as you greet them. This is a very affectionate gesture and it will make them feel relaxed.

Hand holding is so powerful at forming emotional attachments that it is no surprise that in Islam, it is forbidden for a man to hold the hand of a strange woman and vice versa. It is important to note that holding hands does not have to be done in public. Holding hands in public can be nerve-wracking especially for newly married Muslim couples. I advise that it is actually better to hold hands at home. That way it is done more intentionally, and because you are in a safe place, you are able to be more open and feel brave enough to initiate that contact.

Hug often – Hugging is one of the most universal forms of showing love and affection. It is very important in a marriage that you maintain physical closeness often. Remember that it is this physical connection that separates you from being just friends to being a husband and wife. When your spouse returns home from a long day at work, give them a warm embrace. Hold the embrace for a few seconds and really enjoy hugging your spouse. The benefits of hugging are that it causes relaxation and stress relief. You will find that when you hug someone, you automatically take in a deep breath and exhale as your body naturally relaxes.

Cuddling your partner is another way of showing affection. It is essential that you keep close physical contact with your partner especially in the early days as it is this physical closeness that forms a bond that cannot be formed in any other way. Sit next to your partner often and lean on them, put your head on their shoulder and link arms with them. Cuddling can include putting your arm around your wife as she stands in the kitchen making dinner or just laying your head in his lap as he is sat down after prayer. It is natural for human beings to crave closeness with another human. When you love someone, you naturally want to be close to them at all times.

It is completely understandable that at the beginning of your marriage, or if your marriage connection is not good, it will be awkward to do these things. But you must remember that the only way to make it less awkward is to just start doing it and don't think too much about it ! Your spouse will really welcome these little moments of affection and it will have a big impact on their heart. It will also trigger them to be more loving.

Touch – Touching encompasses hugging, holding hands, cuddling, and massage. Human beings crave touch. It is one of the most primal Instincts that we have. Do not be shy to touch your spouse. Examples of this can be simply placing your hand on your partner`s thigh as he is driving. Or perhaps stroking your wife's hair and placing it behind her ears. Be adventurous and touch your spouse when they least expect it. As your marriage develops and your connection becomes stronger, you may find that you touch your spouse without even realising it. When you touch each other often, it really shows a sense of familiarity and comfortability with your spouse. And that is exactly what your spouse should be for you, they should be so familiar to you and you should feel so comfortable with them that they almost become an extension of yourself.

Massage – Massage should definitely be something that you and your spouse enjoy doing together. When your spouse comes back from a long day at work, massage their shoulders or the temples of their head. This will help to relax them and it will become a special thing they look forward to when they come home. Do not forget to repay the favour to your spouse and also give them a massage. When you return home and you know your spouse has been with the children all day, how about you give her a spontaneous massage? It is important to note that when you notice your spouse doing something nice for you, you reciprocate the favour. This will encourage your spouse to do more and it will stop them from feeling as if It is only a one-sided relationship.

Nicknames – Nicknames are a fun way to create your own special moments in your marriage. You can give your spouse a special name or you can use terms like "babe" "habibi" or "darling". We know that our beloved Prophet [S.A.W] had nicknames for his wife Aisha [R.A]. He would call her A'ish or Homayraa . Nicknames show a great sense of familiarity and friendship.

Gifts and surprises. – Buying your spouse gifts is a sure guaranteed way to show that you care about them. It does not have to be expensive gifts, it is more about being aware of your partner and remembering what they like. Anticipate their needs and surprise them with what they love. Why not buy them a bunch of their favourite flowers randomly or maybe their favourite bar of chocolate. Remember, it's the little things. One of the most affectionate things you can do for your partner is to show them that you know them well. To show them that you know the little things they like and their little quirks. This will definitely open up your spouse's heart to loving you more.

Pillow talk – The term pillow talk is used to describe the time spent talking once you get into bed at night. Try to go to bed a little earlier so you can lay in bed together and you'll be surprised how the conversation flows. Talk about anything and everything. Talk about your deepest fears, reminisce about the past, and plan your future together. You will find that at these late hours of the night, in the blanket of darkness, you are able to open up and be more vulnerable to your spouse. The bond that this will create between you will be remarkable. Think of your spouse as that one person that you can share with all your hopes and worries. Someone that is with you for life to be your supporter and helper in every way.

Make their favourite meal – You may have heard the saying that the way to a man's heart is through his stomach. There could some truth to that. Cooking for your spouse a special meal is a really sweet and caring way of letting them know that you love them and want to make them happy. If you know a particular food that your spouse likes, it's good to take some time out and cook it for them.

A great marriage is about making each other feel special and important - cooking your partner their favourite meal is one of the ways to do so. Many people associate a home-cooked meal with love and affection. This is due to the fact that we grow up with our mothers cooking for us and making sure we have eaten well every single day. That is why you often hear people remembering their mothers cooking with great fondness. It was not just about the taste, it was also about the feelings of love and care that those memories bring back. When you cook for your husband or prepare for him food, it shows deep care and concern for him. It makes him feel loved and cared for and isn't that what we are all seeking.

Love notes – in this day and age, many have neglected the art of handwriting a letter or a note. A handwritten note is something so precious and it shows that you put effort into doing it. It's a great idea to have sticky notes so you can write your spouse little compliments and leave them in places to surprise them. Maybe before you leave for work in the morning you could leave a note in the kitchen cupboard saying "I love you". Or maybe you can make your husband lunch for work and put a little note in there. This will keep him thinking about you all day and he will feel loved. Small efforts like this may seem so insignificant but it is such things that keep the spark alive between two people in a marriage. It always comes down to the small things.

Be excited to see your spouse – When your spouse returns home from work, It is important to greet them at the door and show them that you are excited to see them and happy that they are home. Acknowledge their return and do not keep doing what you were doing. You should leave everything else and welcome them home. This may seem like a small gesture but it will have a great impact on your marriage. It will show your spouse that they are important and valued. Sit with your spouse and ask them how their day was. Maybe pour them a glass of water and listen as they tell you about their day.

Spend time together – We live in a very fast-paced world. As we grow older, we have many commitments and it can be easy to get lost In the hustle for financial security - and in doing so we often neglect our relationships. You must realise that your marriage is a priority. Do not get so occupied in your job that you neglect the very reason why you are working so hard. Prioritising your marriage means that even on busy days, you still manage to get ten minutes to call your wife and speak to her during your lunch break. Or perhaps you pick her up from work even if you are tired and it may mean that you get home a little later.

Show your spouse that they are important to you by sacrificing your time and energy for them. Sometimes you may have other plans but when your spouse asks you to do something for them, you can change those plans just to show your spouse that they are valuable to you. For example, you could finish work early to take your wife to an appointment that you know is important to her. The truth is that marriage is a sacrifice. Sometimes you may have to sacrifice what you love in order to please your spouse but you will always get more in return in the long run. You will also get rewarded by Allaah.

It is important to spend time together with your spouse because that is the only way that you will get to know each other. How can you know somebody when you do not spend time with them? And how can you love somebody that you do not know? No doubt that sometimes in life we get very preoccupied and that is understandable. But you must communicate this to your spouse so they do not feel neglected. A simple conversation can be all that is needed to explain to your spouse that you love and care for them so much but it is a bit hectic at work that is why you have not been available.

It is important to always communicate your feelings so there is no confusion. When we do not communicate our feelings, we allow our spouse to make up a scenario in their mind which could lead to negative feelings. You may think that your spouse already knows that you are working hard for a better future for both of you, but we as human beings need reassurance and reminding often. Let your spouse know that you have been busy lately and it hurts that you haven't been able to spend as much time together. Why not plan a day off work and tell them that you want to spend the day with them because you miss them so dearly.

9. Dating Each Other

One of the most precious pieces of advice given in regard to marriage is to make sure that you continue to date each other for as long as you are married. Dating each other is important in any marriage but even more so in an Islamic marriage. This is because, in Islam, men and women are to have no private interactions before marriage. So they do not get a chance to get to know each other on a personal or romantic level before the marriage. Then after the nikah, many couples will begin living together immediately. This can be a big change for many people. When you date each other, you allocate specific time to get to know each other on a romantic level.

Put simply, it is important to date each other so that you can fall in love. When you go on a date, you create a space for romance and love to develop, and every time you go on a date, you reignite that love. I believe one of the main reasons why marriages fail within the Muslim community is because the couple does not make the effort to build love for each other after marriage. You must make an effort to build that love and connection after you are married. Do not expect that connection to magically appear, rather you have to put effort into building it. One of the ways to do so is by dating each other.

As women, it is within our nature to want to be chased and pursued by a man, just like it is in the nature of men to want to pursue a woman. It is the role of the husband to pursue his wife, to woo her, romance her, and make her feel desired. Going on dates should be a regular routine in your marriage. It is best to have a date once a week. As a minimum, it should be at least once every two weeks but not to be left any longer than that.

Having a date with your husband or wife is not the same as simply going out to lunch or dinner. A date is a specific time set aside for you two to get closer and connect to each other. That should be the intention of both of you. You should focus on your spouse and give them your undivided attention. Do not speak about the usual things that you do every day such as the children or your job. Instead, you should put your attention on each other. Ask each other how you are, make jokes, and be fully present in the moment. Do not go on a date with your spouse and spend the whole time looking at your phone and not being present. That is simply a waste.

A suggestion that I often give couples is to ask each other specific questions on the date. When on a date with your spouse, it is better to have targeted conversations. This can be in the form of structured questions which are designed to connect you on a deeper level. You will find 30 such questions at the back of this book that you can ask each other on a date. These questions have been specifically written to spark deep conversation. Some will be fun, some will be serious and some will be romantic. Take it in turns asking each other questions and really focus on answering in-depth. Each question has been designed to be a conversation on its own so do not rush through the questions. These questions will help you to get to know each other on a deeper level. You will begin to realise each other's morals and vulnerabilities which will inevitably form a deep bond between the two of you.

Date Ideas

Having a date with your spouse can be done in many different ways. The great thing about a date is that it does not have to involve a lot of money or planning. For example, you can go to a fancy restaurant but you can also have a small picnic in the park.

The important thing is that you set aside time to spend together building your relationship. It should be clear in both your minds that you are not just going out to eat, no, you are going out to build a bond and strengthen your marriage. Having a date does not require that you spend a lot of money. Sometimes the best dates are the ones where you just go out for a cup of coffee. Below are some great ideas.

Picnic – This is not an ordinary picnic, this is a romantic picnic. Gather some food together, make it something light and picnic style. Find a quiet spot in the park, lay a cloth, sit down and just talk and eat. The fresh air can help to relax you and the sounds of nature can create a serene environment. Pick one topic to talk about. For example, something interesting about each other that you did not know. Maybe something about your childhood. Keep the phones away so that you are able to give each other your full attention.

Stargazing – This one will require you to go outside at night to sit and watch the stars. You will be amazed at how much you open up when the world is all dark around you. It gives a sense of just the two of you against the world. Allow yourself to be vulnerable and open up about things that maybe no one else knows about you. One of the most powerful ways to build a bond in a married couple is vulnerability. You can even bring a blanket and cuddle up together as it might get a bit chilly. Give this one a try and am sure you will love it. If you have a balcony, you can even do it on there or simply park the car and stay inside it with a warm drink and talk.

Restaurant – Going out to eat is the most common type of date and it is for a good reason. We all love food, food makes us happy and so it's a perfect place to start to build your relationship. Find a nice quiet table and sit opposite each other. Again, it is very important to be present and remove all other distractions like your mobile phone. Talk to each other and listen to each other. What do you love about your spouse? what do you love most about being married? Compliment your spouse and don't forget to laugh together. Maybe talk about the things you were worried about before marriage and am sure you'll find that your spouse had similar worries.

At home – A date at home is a really great idea, especially for Muslim couples. When you have a date at home, the wife can dress however she likes. Because you will be staying at home, she does not have to worry about being in hijab and this means that she can wear a nice outfit, makeup, and even perfume. The home also provides a safe environment where you may feel more comfortable expressing your selves. All attention will be on each other as there will be no distractions in the form of music or talking from other people. Why not prepare a meal together? Perhaps you can plan ahead and get the ingredients ready for an adventurous meal that is new to you both. You can then prepare the meal together. This will be a fun bonding experience.

✽ ✽ ✽

10. Beautifying And Complimenting

Beautifying yourself for your spouse is another romantic thing to do. When you make an effort to beautify yourself for your spouse, they feel special and that you really want to please them. It is widely known that men are highly visual creatures. They are easily aroused by what they see and it is therefore important for the wife to ensure she looks good for her husband.

It is important to note that beautifying yourself for your husband is not a bad thing. Often times society will make a woman feels as though saving herself for her husband is a negative thing. When both spouses are happily married, then it is enjoyable to beautify yourself for each other and to please each other in every way. When a woman loves a man, she is inclined to want to beautify herself for him and that does not make her oppressed nor does it mean that he `owns` her. Rather, the Muslim woman knows that the only one that owns her is Allaah, and that she gets rewarded for everything she does in her marriage.

Fake It Till You Make It

Ladies, remember that confidence is attractive! So once you have beautified yourself and have put on your enticing clothes, you must act the part! Stroll around the house in confidence, as if you are the most beautiful woman alive! Confidence is very alluring and it will make you appear even more attractive to your spouse.

When he gives you a compliment, accept it and don't be shy. You may feel a little bashful to wear revealing clothes, especially in the early days of marriage, but you can always fake the confidence until you finally get it.

Beautifying is not just restricted to wives, we know the famous saying of Ibn Abbas [R.A] who said, "Verily, I love to beautify myself for my wife, just as I love for her to beautify herself for me, due to the saying of Allah Almighty: They have rights similar to those over them." (2:228) al-Sunan al-Kubrá 14264. So it is important that the husband also makes the effort to beautify himself and wear clothes that will please his wife. He must make necessary efforts to appear looking attractive to his wife. This may mean going to the gym to maintain his physique or grooming his hair and beard.

Let The Compliments Flow

Before a woman gets married, beautifying herself is often done for fun or when there is a party to attend. However, after marriage, beautifying herself becomes a duty. Of course, it is not possible to be beautified at all times, and it would be unrealistic to expect women to be looking flawless at all times. This is especially true when a woman has children or when she works outside the home. A great tip for the wives would

It is so important for the husband to compliment his wife, that we even have an exception in the Deen to *lie* about it if necessary. The Prophet [S.A.W] said, "it is not lawful to lie except in three cases: Something the man tells his wife to please her ..." Jami` at-Tirmidhi 1939. For example, a man may say to his wife "you are the most beautiful woman I have ever seen". That may not be true, but it is allowed to make such statements to please each other. The same applies to a wife lying to her husband in such a manner.

The truth is that we all love compliments, especially women. Muslim women cannot beautify themselves when going outside of the home. Therefore, when your wife beautifies herself for you, you must show her that you are pleased because nobody else gets to see her like that. It is also important to note that it can be nerve-wracking (especially at the beginning of marriage) for a Muslim woman to dress in enticing clothes because this is not something she was used to doing. So when she does make the effort to do so, make sure to go overboard with the compliments!

Notice the little details, for example, the new earrings or the new lipstick that she is wearing. Anything that you see that you like, let your wife know about it! Do not keep it in your mind because then she will never know and automatically she may assume that you don't like it. You will be surprised how much it can increase your wife's self-esteem and confidence when you compliment her. Complimenting her will encourage her to do more. Be very verbally expressive with your compliments.

Complimenting your wife is something that should be done frequently. Compliment her on everything. Compliment her on her cooking, cleaning, looking after the children, and everything else! You must show her that you are her biggest fan and let her know that you notice and appreciate all that she does. Really put effort into complimenting your wife.

You should also let your wife hear you complimenting her and speaking good of her to your family and other people. This will make your wife feel special, loved, and valued.

An important note to point out is that many women forget to compliment their husbands. Or maybe they feel that they do not need to do so. It is important to compliment your husband on his looks as well as his other good qualities. He will feel loved and appreciated. Compliment him on his body physique and on his strength. Let him know that you feel safe and protected around him. He will appreciate you so much more and see that his hard work does not go unnoticed.

* * *

11. Intimacy

When we speak about forming a secure marriage bond, we cannot neglect the topic of intimacy. When we speak about intimacy, we are referring to sex and all that leads up to it. Although we cannot say that intimacy is the most important aspect of a marriage, we can certainly say that a marriage cannot survive without it. Intimacy plays a very big role in forming a strong marriage bond. It is important to note that there are fundamental differences in the way that men and women process intimacy. It is important to understand these differences so that you can understand your spouse better and know how to best please them.

The Differences

Lets discuss the ways that men and women are different in regards to intimacy. For women, arousal and desire are mostly processed in the brain. Whilst for men, desire, and arousal are linked to the physiological effect of looking at a woman's body. A man can easily be aroused by simply looking at a woman's body, but for a woman, it is more complicated. This natural disconnect between the two genders can bring rise to many problems because they simply do not understand each other. Women often do not recognise the importance of intimacy in marriage and this quickly leaves men feeling unloved and frustrated.

Studies have shown that the arousal of women is linked to

feeling loved and desired by their partner, as well as being stress-free. In order for a woman to be fully open and comfortable during intimacy, she must first feel completely safe in the love of her husband. Worries, stress, and anxiety can also affect a woman's sexual desire. It is therefore important to make sure that your wife feels desired, loved and is stress free. One of the ways to make your wife feel desired is by complimenting her often. Compliment her throughout the day, not just at the time of intimacy.

An important issue to address when it comes to the issue of intimacy is that neither of the spouses should ever insult or make fun of each other`s physical appearance. Sometimes a comment can be made as a joke but it will deeply hurt your partner. Once a hurtful comment is made, it is very hard to take it back.

Oftentimes, husbands will complain about their wife not wanting to engage in intimacy or they will complain of their wife's lack of enthusiasm during intimacy. The problem is always much deeper than just the act of sex itself. The problem will usually originate from a deeper issue within the marriage which is making the woman feel unsettled. It is only when a woman feels completely safe in her husband's love that she can fully be open and reciprocal during intimacy.

We have seen that for men, desire and arousal are linked to what they see of a woman's body. Men are highly visual creatures. Knowing this, it is a duty upon the wife to make sure that she dresses in a manner that will please her husband. A great tip is to ask your husband what he wants you to wear. Or maybe the husband can surprise the wife with what he would like her to wear for him. It is important to ensure that the sexual desires of your husband are met as long as they fall within the realms of what is permissible in Islam. The same applies to the husband who must ensure that he fulfills the desires of his wife.

Tragic Mistake

It is often the case that women do not recognise the importance of intimacy in marriage. This is a tragic mistake that quickly leaves men feeling unloved and perhaps even angry. I call this a tragic mistake because it is often the beginning of the end of a marriage. This issue can normally be solved very easily with communication. Both spouses have to work together to overcome this issue.

As a husband, you should not expect your wife to understand your needs without you telling her. If you feel that you are not happy in this area, you must communicate this with your wife clearly. Make it clear to her, for example, that you need to be intimate more often, or that you would like her to make more of an effort during intimacy. Please ensure you are clear and direct in your communication. Do not joke about it or make it to be a small issue because she may not take you seriously. You have to be very clear and direct in your speech. If you find it difficult to speak about this issue, you can write down what you would like to say and give your wife a note.

Allaah has created men and women so differently in this area, that you may find your wife was not aware of how severely this was affecting you.

Forming Bonds

One of the easiest ways for a wife to build a bond with her husband is through intimacy. It is well known that men usually have a stronger desire for physical intimacy than women. So the wife must do her best to always be available for intimacy when her husband needs her. This will please the husband and strengthen the marriage connection.

In a well-known Hadeeth, Abū Hurayrah [R.A] narrated from

the Prophet [S.A.W] : "If a husband calls his wife to go to bed with him and she refuses and the husband spends the night in anger [at her refusal], then the angels curse her till dawn". (Bukhārī: No. 2998). This Hadeeth shows us the importance of fulfilling the needs of your husband sexually. It shows us that it is sinful should a wife refuse to have intimate relations with her husband without good cause.

Allaah has described the spouses as being like "garments" to each other. Allaah said in the Holy Qur`an " They are your garments and you are their garments." (2;187) This is a powerful metaphor to show the intimate closeness that a husband and wife have. Your garment is almost an extension of you. It provides cover, protection of your most vulnerable parts and it is comforting.

An important issue to discuss is that often husbands may not realise that their wives also have needs that need to be met. Unfortunately, some husbands do not realise the importance of fulfilling their wife's needs when it comes to intimacy. And I believe our communities do not put enough effort into addressing this issue. Did you know that a woman may be able to divorce her husband because of a lack of sexual fulfilment? This is enough to show us the importance of this issue.

Intimacy is heavily linked to emotion in women, and so it is the case that when a woman is intimate with a man, she forms an emotional bond with him. So put effort into making sure that your wife is pleased during intimacy and this will facilitate in forming a strong emotional bond between you two. If there are any issues in this department and any help is needed, it is important to discuss this together. You will find your spouse to be open and understanding.

Effect of upbringing - shyness

Growing up in Muslim homes, many of us may have the view that sex is something to be shy about, never to be spoken of, and to be avoided at all costs. This is a result of the great effort our parents put into raising us to remain chaste and obedient to Allaah. There is no blame on our parents for this, and in fact, they are to be applauded for it. We ask Allaah to have mercy upon our parents. However, with that in mind, one of the challenges Muslim women face once they are married is replacing the notion of sex as being shameful and accepting it as something that is good. Actually, not just good, but also something that is required and that you get rewarded for doing. I must say Muslim men don't seem to struggle too much with accepting that notion, because well, that's how Allaah created them.

The point to be made here is that Muslim husbands must be prepared for their wife to be shy and perhaps even appear to be unwilling to participate in intimacy. Women will vary in degree with their level of shyness. Some women may need only a day to get over the shyness, whilst other women might open up slowly over weeks, months, or even years. What you should do as a husband is to reassure her – constantly. Yes, you have to keep reassuring her that you love her, desire her, and that she is safe with you. When you show your wife that you are willing to be patient with her, she will appreciate you greatly and it will really cultivate a special bond between you two. As we mentioned earlier, it is only when a woman feels safe in the love of a man that she will fully be able to let go of her inhibitions and be her best self.

A tip to help the sisters who may be overly shy is to remember that it is permissible and actually the duty of a wife to be intimate with her husband. Did you know that the original literal meaning of the word `nikah` is `sexual intercourse`? All the righteous predecessors who were married also did the same and there is nothing bad about it.

It is also advised to wear clothes that are revealing around the house once you are married, this will certainly help in developing your confidence and making you less shy. Perhaps your shyness is linked to low self-esteem or even a past trauma that you haven't healed from? Please seek help or open up to your spouse. Most importantly, make dua to Allaah and ask Him to help you and make things easy for you.

Talk About It!

As a couple, you should work towards normalising the conversation of intimacy between each other. Let it be something that you talk about together often, even outside of the bedroom. Make your own jokes about it, send each other text messages about it, and so on. Isn't it amazing that Allah has allowed us to have this private section of our lives that we share with just one other person? It is certainly one of the best ways to build a connection with each other. Remember that Intimacy is supposed to be fun! so laugh about it and do your best to make each other comfortable and reassured. Over time, you will lose your inhibitions and open up.

To conclude on intimacy, we must mention the importance of hygiene. It is essential that both spouses maintain the highest levels of hygiene. It Is important that your spouse feels confident in your level of hygiene. Your spouse should feel confident to be close to you at any time and be able to trust that you will be clean and have no unpleasant odours.

Hygiene takes into account all body areas, from head to toe. Lack of proper hygiene is something that can really negatively affect your intimacy and therefore your marriage. If your hygiene is not to the highest standard, your spouse will not want to be close to you. Over time, your spouse may even begin to be repulsed by you.

This is a topic that can be very difficult to address with your spouse. It is a sensitive topic. If you notice that your spouse is lacking in their hygiene, I would recommend first that you make dua to Allaah to rectify that for them.

If matters persist and become unbearable, you can speak to your spouse about the issue or perhaps write them a message. Begin by apologising and acknowledging that it is going to be an awkward conversation. Reassure your spouse that you love them dearly and are attracted to them. Then tell them the issue using gentle words. Your spouse may be defensive at first, but they should cool down and accept that it's better that you were the one to speak about the issue to them instead of a stranger.

A tip I have to recommend from the Sunnah is to be consistent in using the siwak to clean one's teeth and mouth.

It is important to know that if your spouse notices that your hygiene is lacking, it is very unlikely that they will say anything to you about it. This is because it is such a sensitive topic so they may find themselves unable to ever bring it up. You must therefore be very self-critical of your own self in this area. Always maintain the highest standards of hygiene possible.

The topic of intimacy is one that requires a lot of communication. You must speak openly about it in your marriage. Be brutally honest and explain to your spouse what exactly you need from them in this area of your marriage. Will it be uncomfortable to speak about at first? Of course. But I promise it will get easier.

✻ ✻ ✻

12. Appreciation And Gratitude

It is important to make sure that you show gratitude to your spouse and you show them that you appreciate them. Marriage is a union between two people where each person is doing their best every day to show love and care for the other person. Sometimes the things we do in marriage become so normal to us that we do them subconsciously. It is important to remind your spouse often that you see what they do and that you appreciate the things they do for you every day, the small and the big things.

When someone shows gratitude, we are inclined to keep doing the good we are doing and to do even more for them. An example of showing gratitude is thanking your spouse for going to work every day. Let them know that you see them when they wake up early in the morning to go out and work, regardless of what the weather is like and even when they are sick. Let them know that you realise they are doing this for your family and your future and that you are so appreciative of it. You should allow yourself to be vulnerable and make your words soft and full of emotion. Your spouse will feel so motivated and understood. Strive to make your marriage a sanctuary of positivity and support.

Often overlooked is the mother who stays at home and looks after children. If your spouse stays at home and looks after your children, it is important to let them know that you value them and that you do not disregard what they do. Showing gratitude is more than just words, it is also In actions. Why not allow your wife to have a lie-in on alternate weekends so she can rest? let her know that you see her with the children every day and you appreciate so much what she is doing to raise those children. Sometimes after a long day at home with the children, all your wife needs to hear are a few words of love and encouragement to liven her up and have her ready for the next day.

Show your spouse that you appreciate them not just for what they do, but also for who they are. Words such as "You are the person I have been praying for" or "You are my peace" are so important and they hit deeper than any other words could. So many times we feel this way about our spouses but we do not express those feelings. What a waste, because if you do not say the words out of your mouth, your spouse will never know how you feel. When you begin to express such beautiful words to your spouse, they will also be inclined to do the same.

Another way to make your spouse feel appreciated is by talking good about them to other people. You should be your spouse's biggest fan. You should let your family and her/his family know how good he is to you and that he/she treats you well. This will not only please your spouse but also their family members.

Take note that the first step to gratitude and appreciation is acknowledgment. You must learn to acknowledge even the small things. Do not take your spouse for granted – be grateful to have them and be grateful for everything that they do. And most importantly, let them know that you are grateful for them.

* * *

13. Love Who I Love

Do you want to know a shortcut in creating love in your marriage? Love the ones whom your spouse loves!

One of the best parts of marriage is that you meet someone new and you get a fresh chance at starting a new life. It's so exciting to think of all the things you will achieve together in the future InshaAllaah. A big aspect we have to remember is that your spouse had a life before they met you. Do not neglect that part of your spouse's life. Do not neglect their family and their childhood experiences and how they grew up.

One of the best ways of building a bond with your spouse and creating love is by showing interest in who they are. Their family and childhood are who they are, their childhood experiences and family shaped them to be the person they are today. When you show interest in the family of your spouse, it will make your spouse feel that you are really interested in getting to know them on a deeper level.

One of the first things to discuss with your new husband or wife is their childhood and upbringing. You should talk about everything! Which school did they go to? Who was their best friend? Tell each other stories about the times you got into trouble as young children. Talk to each other about the funny family stories that happened growing up. There should never be a dull moment as there is so much to talk about. What was your spouse's dream job as a child? Which university did they attend? In this way, you will get to know your spouse and build a wholesome relationship. You will get to know your spouse in a way that no one else knows them. You will know what they are like as a brother/sister, a friend, a daughter/son and also as a spouse.

When you speak to your spouse about their childhood and upbringing, you may begin to understand why they are the way they are. For example, your spouse may have had some childhood trauma, maybe they went through a testing time. It is important that you are supportive of your spouse when discussing such fragile issues and that you show them that you are there for them.

Great emphasis is put on the importance of showing care and concern to the family members of your spouse. You must love those whom your spouse loves. His/ her parents are the dearest people to her so show her that you care about them and she will know that you are a kind-hearted person. I have had the experience of speaking with a woman who divorced her husband. She said that one of the red flags she noticed early on was that her husband showed no interest in her family or in who she was as a person.

It is essential to show interest in your spouse's parents. Show your wife/husband that you care about their parents and their well-being. Ask often how they are health wise and in general. Recommend to her that you visit them often. Offer to buy them groceries and bring them to them. Ask them about how they are coping with old age or with their livelihood.

You can also develop your own relationship with your spouse's parents. Do not always wait for her to be around for you to call them. Find some time out of your busy schedule to contact her parents and offer them help - you do not need your wife's approval to be good to her parents and it will make her even more happy that you thought about her parents on your own accord.

If your spouse's parents live abroad, ask about them often and call them. If they live in poverty or are less fortunate than you are, then make sure to set up some charity funds for them that you send to them periodically. Show Kindness and concern when the parents of your spouse are unwell. During important occasions like Eid and Ramadhan, it is important to help out the less fortunate parents and relatives. This will show you to be not only caring and considerate but also respectful.

Your spouse`s siblings are another important part of their life. You must remember that when your wife married you, she left her family and siblings behind who she had lived with her entire life. Some women will even move to a different country to be with you. It is important that you show her that you care for her siblings by forming a friendship with them. If your wife has brothers, it is incumbent that you form a friendship bond with them. Make an effort to contact them and build a brotherhood. There are many ways to form a bond with them, this can be through even something as simple as meeting up to play football on the weekend! If your wife's brothers are young, then show interest in their education, maybe help them to find a job or teach them the Deen.

We must emphasise here the importance of being genuine when doing all these acts. Remember that marriage is an 'Ibaadah', or act of worship. So do all these acts for the sake of Allaah and not only will you please your spouse but you will also please Allaah. Doing things for the sake of Allaah is the best way to do things. Why? Because you are not doing them to show off or because you expect praise, rather you are doing them out of the goodness of your heart.

If your husband has sisters, why not plan a day out so you can get to know each other better. Or maybe surprise your husband and invite them over for dinner one night. It will fill your husband's heart with joy and pride to see you getting along well with his sisters or family members who are so dear to him.

If your wife has nieces and nephews it is important that you also show love and care to them. The Prophet [S.A.W] said that "The maternal aunt is of the same status as the mother." Classed as saheeh by al-Albaani in Saheeh Abi Dawood. This means that your wife will love her nephews and nieces dearly almost as if they are her own children. Show her that you care about those whom she cares about and this will solidify a good bond between you two.

Step Children

An important issue to discuss in this chapter is that of stepchildren. Many of us will get married to someone who already has children. I have failed to find words powerful enough to express how important it is to love those children well. Show them a lot of love and care. Look after them just like you would look after your own. For women who have children and then remarry, this issue is very important in the forming of a strong bond between them and their new spouse. Perhaps for many women, it is more important to them that you love their child even more than you love them. The love of a mother to her child is self-sacrificial, she would easily sacrifice her happiness for her children.

It is not enough to just acknowledge the children and not pay them much attention. No, rather, you must make a substantial effort to get to know them, interact with them, spend time with them and support them both financially and emotionally. It goes without saying that the exact same rules apply to a woman who marries a man who has children.

14. Support And Care

One of the things that are guaranteed in life is that there will be difficult times. Allaah has told us in the Qur`an that He will put us through tests. One of the most beautiful things about marriage is that you always have someone with you to share those difficult times. Someone who will be there to support you and hold you tight when life becomes difficult.

It goes without saying that when your spouse is going through a difficult time, you should do your utmost to be their ultimate pillar of strength and support. You must be aware that your spouse will be expecting you to be their number one source of support and strength and you must be prepared to do just that. In order for you to be supportive of your spouse, you will need to have sympathy, as well as empathy. Empathy is the deeper level of sympathy. It is being able to imagine yourself in the position of another person and truly feel what they feel. When you have empathy for your spouse, you are able to support them well because you can imagine yourself in their situation.

When your spouse is going through a difficult time, be open and let them know that it hurts you when they are upset. It is important that you never dismiss the feelings of your spouse. Something which your spouse may view as very difficult may not appear to be so difficult for you, but you must not dismiss their feelings. When you dismiss your spouse's feelings, then they will no longer feel comfortable confiding in you.

Difficult times can vary greatly in degree. We can never know what life will throw at us. Some examples of challenging times in your lives could be financial difficulties, sickness of a spouse, loss of a family member, pregnancy and child-raising, and many more. Some difficult times may affect you together as a couple and some may affect only one spouse. The key to getting through these times successfully is effective communication. This is the time when you need to make sure that your communication is fully open and present. It is important to establish good communication in your relationship right from the beginning so that during difficult times, your spouse feels comfortable to open up to you. Below are some ways to show support to your spouse.

Ways To Show Support

Make sincere dua for your spouse and let them know that you are doing so.

Simply sit with your spouse and hold them and talk to them. Do not be afraid to show your spouse your emotions. Often when we see somebody that we love crying, we will feel like crying as well and that's ok.

Ask your spouse how they are feeling and let them know that you are there for them. Let them know that it hurts you to see them so upset. Be verbally expressive. Remember, if you don't say it, your spouse will have no way of knowing.

Depending on the severity of the situation, you may need to take a day off from work or maybe even more time if it is required. Show your spouse that you are ready to drop everything to support them. And if you are not able to, then explain to them why in detail, and let them know that if it were up to you, you would have been with them immediately.

Find ways to make your spouse happy. This can be with the smallest of things or with a bigger gesture. Simple things such as buying flowers, chocolates, or a cup of coffee could really help to brighten up your spouse.

It is important to show your spouse that you care about them, that you have mercy on them, and that it affects you when they are unwell or unhappy. When your spouse is sick, look after them well and lessen the load of duties they have to do. For example, if you know that your wife is sick, it would be caring to ask her not to cook, and instead, you buy food or come home and prepare food for her. This will make your spouse feel loved and also that you appreciate her for the things she does when she is in good health.

Difficult times are really a test of strength in your marriage and they will either break you or make you stronger. You may be surprised that a difficult time can really strengthen your marriage bond. When people go through hardships, they always remember the ones that were there to support them during that difficult time. Therefore, you must do your best to support your spouse and be there for them during their lowest times.

✳ ✳ ✳

15. Working Through Problems

Marriage is a union between two people, and because people are not perfect, we can also expect that no marriage will be perfect. Yes, there will be days when your spouse does something which is displeasing to you. They may even say something which will be hurtful. The way to get through these difficult times in marriage is, first of all, to ask Allaah for help and guidance. Secondly, it is through communication and forgiveness.

Forgiveness

Forgiveness and overlooking mistakes are a major part of marriage. You will find that marriage involves working through a lot of micro arguments. It also involves a lot of patience and perseverance. You must be willing to fight for your marriage. There will be times when your spouse will be in a bad mood, perhaps they had a difficult day at work or they received some bad news, they could then take out their frustrations on you. The best way to deal with this is patience and calmness. Allaah tells us in the Holy Quran that "Good and evil cannot be equal. Repel evil with what is better and your enemy will become as close as an old and valued friend" 41: 34. So respond to your partner with calmness and goodness and this will only strengthen your relationship.

There is a beautiful saying from a companion called Abu Dardaa [R.A] who said to his wife: "If you see me angry, calm me down, and if I see you angry, I will calm you down, otherwise it will be too difficult to live together."

Many disagreements can be avoided if your words are planned carefully. For example, if you feel that your husband doesn't spend enough time with you, instead of approaching him with blame, why not try a different approach. For example, instead of saying " you never take me out to eat, we never spend any time together" you could try saying instead "I would love it if we went out together just me and you, I miss spending time with you". When it is phrased in this manner, it is more likely that your husband will receive it in a positive way and want to do it.

If you find a trait in your spouse that you do not like, try to think of something else that you do like and focus on that trait. A Hadith comes to mind where Abu Huraira reported that the Messenger of Allah [S.A.W] said, "A believing man does not despise a believing woman. If he finds something in her character he dislikes, he will be pleased by something else." Ṣaḥīḥ Muslim 1469. This Hadith encourages us to focus on the strength that your spouse has and focus on the benefits of these strengths. Pray to Allaah to remove that bad trait from your spouse and to make the two of you compatible.

It is always important to address any issues immediately or as soon as possible. For example, if your spouse says something hurtful to you, you should pull them up on it immediately and tell them exactly what they said and how it made you feel. Use direct language that expresses your feelings. So you might say "When you said that to me, I felt very hurt. It made me feel as though you don't care about me. Or perhaps you could ask "what were your intentions in saying that to me?" or maybe you could simply say "It really hurts when you do that, please do not do that again." Whilst it is true that marriage involves compromising and accommodating, it is also important to withhold certain boundaries and make it clear to your spouse the things that you are not willing to accept.

Know Your Own Flaws

It is also good to be self-critical of your own characteristics. When a problem arises with your spouse, first look into yourself and see If there is anything you could have done to contribute to this problem. This will help you to stay grounded and not to get too angry. Put effort into understanding yourself and your flaws. Once you understand your own flaws, then you can be more understanding of others' flaws too.

Where possible, try your best to adapt to your spouse so that you make life easier for both of you. This may mean making compromises at times so that you maintain the peace. Do this for the sake of Allaah and it will be rewarded greatly in the hereafter. The Prophet [S.A.W] said " I guarantee a house in Jannah for one who gives up arguing, even if he is in the right"... Sunan Abu Dawud. Teach yourself that you do not have to win every argument. Sometimes letting things go so that you can maintain peace is better than proving a point. In fact, if you notice that you always win every argument with your spouse, that could be a sign that perhaps you are being pushy and overwhelming your spouse. Nobody is always right all the time.

Know that there is no perfect marriage out there and you should never compare your marriage to other marriages. How many times have we seen marriages which appear to be perfect on the outside but in reality, the marriage is not a happy one. Remember that the grass is not always greener on the other side, rather it is greener where it is watered. Ultimately there is no perfect person in this word, and so your spouse will never be perfect.

It is important that even during times of disagreement, you still maintain respect for each other. There are certain boundaries that should never be crossed. You should never divulge the secrets of your spouse or use against them something which they told you in confidence. Even in anger, do not insult your spouse or call them abusive names. Remember that once said, words cannot be taken back. Even though your spouse may forgive you, they could be slowly building resentment in their heart. It is important to always return and apologise.

Most marriages do not break down due to a major issue. It is normally due to smaller issues that were left neglected, and over time they caused a larger issue. This is because there was no effective communication between the spouses. With that in mind, It is important that when you do something hurtful to your spouse, you apologize and show remorse for what you have done. Even if it may seem insignificant, do not attempt to brush it under the rug and expect your spouse to just get over it. Rather, you should show remorse and talk about it to your spouse.

Hormones

A final note to add to this chapter would be to talk about hormones. For centuries, it has been a joke to talk about the fact that women have different moods at different times of the month, and particularly in pregnancy. It is often funny when we speak about mood swings and the like. It's important to know that scientifically speaking, hormones have been linked to affecting the mood of women in different ways during different times of the month. The trouble-causing hormones are known as oestrogen and progesterone.

The point to be made here is that both spouses should be considerate and patient with each other. The wife should be aware that during certain times of the month, her mood may change. Therefore she should evaluate her emotions so as not to behave in an unpleasant manner.

Husbands should also take into account the fact that sometimes hormones may affect a woman's mood and character. Does this excuse women and make it ok for them to be temperamental?

Of course not. But does it mean that husbands have a duty to be more patient and understanding? Absolutely. When you notice that your spouse is in a bad mood, or to make up after an argument, follow these three steps;

1. Communicate – Try and talk to your spouse. Ask them what is wrong and ask if they want to talk about anything that may be bothering them. Perhaps throw in a compliment or two, and don`t forget to smile.

If this is not well received, then proceed swiftly to step two.

2. The bribe – This is when you try to cheer up your spouse. There are so many ways to do this. It can be as simple as buying your spouse a chocolate bar, giving it to them, and walking away. Or take them for a drive in the car or a walk to get some fresh air. Why not start talking about a subject that you know they love, or watching a YouTube video about said subject - make sure they can hear the video. For example, the topic could be football or Formula 1, or perhaps makeup or house decoration. Sometimes adding a playful element to difficult situations can be helpful.

3. If all else fails, proceed to step three. This step involves simply being patient and remaining calm. Tell your spouse you'll be there for them when they are ready to talk.

✼ ✼ ✼

16. Pregnancy And Postpartum

One of the main goals of getting married is to have children. Alhamdulilaah children are a massive blessing from Allaah to us. It is incredible to think how much joy those little humans can bring. But with big blessings come big responsibilities. It is important to know that when you have children, the entire dynamic of your relationship will change. Children could either strengthen your marriage and make you happier and better than you were before, or they could be the beginning of the end.

It is important to discuss pregnancy and the effect that it can have on your relationship. This is because pregnancy is one of the most life-changing things that a woman can go through, but it is also something that men often do not understand at all. When a woman becomes pregnant, she will no longer be able to fulfill her duties in the same way that she used to. This is because pregnancy will affect her mentally and physically. It is important that husbands are aware of this so that they know how to best assist their wives in navigating through this time. This is essential in order to avoid misunderstandings and negative effects on the marriage.

Also, some women may get pregnant within a month of getting married. This is great, but it is very early on in your marriage and you still have not had time to get to know each other well. So imagine when the pregnancy hormones come into play, it can ruin your marriage before it`s even started. Unless, of course, you are aware of what to expect and how to deal with the changes.

Even before the child is born, pregnancy will be the first

challenge to your marriage. It is known that when a woman is pregnant, she needs a lot of support. Mental support and physical support. She will need mental support because the change in hormones she will experience as her body grows a human will be major. There will be times that she will feel sad, upset, irritable, and even angry. It is the duty of the husband to be patient with her. He should view that as his part of the child carrying.

Weakness Upon Weakness

Allaah shows us the difficulty of pregnancy and postpartum. In the Glorious Qur`an, Allah uses the words "Wahnan Ala Wahn" to describe the stage of pregnancy and breastfeeding. The root meaning of the Arabic word "wahn" is to be weak and feeble, lax in the joints, broken in energy, to sap the strength, to lose vigour or courage, discouraged, disheartened, worn down etc. Allaah does not call this time period just "wahn", rather "wahnan ala wahn" – weakness UPON weakness. Hardship UPON hardship. All the above things layered in double. (ayeina.com). Notice how the word "wahn" does not just refer to physical symptoms such as weakness, but it also refers to mental symptoms such as "discouraged, disheartened" This shows us that the emotional aspects are also important. Do not overlook them.

It is unfortunate that many men do not understand the impact that pregnancy, childbirth, postpartum, and breastfeeding will have on their wife. This is the time that she will need you the most. It is your duty as the father of the child that you support her in any and every way that she needs. If you are patient with her during this time, she will never forget it. She will forever respect you and remember the good that you did for her. This will form a strong bond between you two.

It is worth mentioning that the magnitude of pregnancy and childbirth is shown in the following Hadith where the Prophet

[SAW] said: "The woman who dies in pregnancy or childbirth is a martyr." Abu Dawood, 3111

✽ ✽ ✽

17. Marriage Review

One of the most important things that you will do in your marriage is to have a marriage review. A marriage review is when you sit with your spouse to evaluate your marriage and discuss the good and the bad.

Most people will have a health check once every year, or a dental check every six months. Even employers like to have a review with their employees to make sure they are doing their best at work and are comfortable. However, many people do not ever review their marriages. Marriages need regular maintenance to keep them working at their best and a marriage review is one way to do that.

A marriage review is recommended to be done every two to six months. During a marriage review, you should have an agenda of the issues that need to be discussed. You should begin by highlighting the things that you are happy about in the marriage. Then you discuss the issues that are not going so well and come up with solutions on how to work through them. You should both be prepared to be fully open with each other. You must also be prepared to receive criticism and not to get angry if your spouse tells you things that you may not be happy to hear. Below are some topics to include in your marriage review.

Marriage Review Topics

Evaluate the religious aspect of your marriage. How is that side of your marriage holding up? Are you helping each other to become better Muslims? Are you doing acts of worship together? Please do not neglect this aspect of your marriage. Remember, we are all on different levels of eman and that's ok, but the important thing is to make sure you are doing something, no matter how small.

Discuss the intimate part of your marriage. How are you both feeling about this aspect of your marriage? Are you both happy and satisfied? Are you both pleased with how often you are engaging in intimacy? It is important to be open and discuss this issue. This is your time to voice any concerns that maybe you were too shy to speak about before.

This would also be a good time to discuss any other relevant topics in your marriage. Talk about the in-laws, the children, finances, housing, etc. Each marriage is unique and you are best placed to know what needs to be discussed in your marriage.

After the marriage review, you must work to meet the goals that you set and to make any changes that you agreed upon. When done correctly, a marriage review will help to strengthen your marriage bond greatly. You do not have to be having problems in your marriage to have a marriage review. It must be done as regular maintenance in order to keep each spouse accountable and make sure you are both happy, comfortable, and on the same page.

❉ ❉ ❉

18. Things To Avoid

There are certain things which you must avoid doing as they will damage your marriage bond. It is important to be cautious not to offend your spouse's feelings. The marriage bond is made up of love, trust, and friendship. Be careful not to break any of those three components as once broken, they can be very difficult to rebuild. Listed below are some things to avoid doing as they will be detrimental to your relationship.

Never make fun of looks or weight. It is never acceptable to make fun of the way your spouse looks or of their weight. Do not try to do this even if it is in a joking manner. Many of us have deep-rooted insecurities and when someone makes fun of those insecurities a line is immediately drawn and resentment begins to build. Chances are that your spouse will not show you that you have offended them, and they may even laugh along with you. But this does not mean that they are pleased with you. Do not make fun of their facial features or make comments which could be interpreted as being offensive.

Avoid making fun of your spouse's body shape or weight. This is particularly important for Muslim women because as we know, the Muslim woman is required to cover her entire body in front of people outside of her family. The only person that gets to view her entire body is her husband. If the husband makes an offensive comment about her body, you can imagine the impact this will have on her. It could damage her self-esteem greatly and leave her feeling insecure.

Do not mock your spouse in the way they speak. It may be that your spouse has a different accent or they are not as articulate as you are. Please do not mock them and make them any less about this.

Do not question their intelligence. Do not make your spouse feel as though you are degrading their intellect. There may be situations where your spouse will take longer to understand things, you must be patient with your spouse and not insult them.

Do not embarrass your spouse in front of other people. Do not make a joke on their behalf. Even if they laugh, they will just be hiding their true feelings to avoid embarrassment. You should always be on the side of your spouse especially in front of other people.

Do not expose the secrets of your spouse to other people. Not only will this break the trust in your relationship, but it is also a major sin before Allaah.

Do not make your spouse feel left out when you are with your family and friends. Sometimes we may do this subconsciously as we get carried away enjoying ourselves with our family and friends. You must remember to include your spouse. If you speak a different language that your spouse does not understand, do not speak that language when your spouse is around. Doing so will make your spouse to feel left out.

The easiest way to create resentment in your marriage is to compare your spouse to another person. Do not compare your spouse to someone else. It does not matter if it is a small or big situation. This will make your spouse feel unappreciated, as though you are not satisfied with them. Many husbands tend to compare their wives to other people without realising the magnitude of it. Do not compare your wife's cooking and do not overly praise another woman`s cooking in the presence of your wife. Do not compare the way that your wife raises your children to the way that other children are raised. This will leave your wife feeling attacked and as though she is not good enough.

In a similar manner, it is crucial for the wife not to compare her husband to any other man. A good husband will try his utmost best to make his wife happy every single day. When you compare him to other men in situations that he has no control over, this will utterly crush him and make him feel inadequate. Over time, this will cause a great divide in your marriage.

Do not gossip about your spouse to anybody else or tell of their bad faults. Gossiping is a major sin before Allaah. Whatever you gossip about your spouse will always come back to them. Now imagine how betrayed they will feel when they find out that you have been speaking badly of them behind their back. If you have an issue with your spouse, you must address them directly. If it reaches a point where you believe you need outside assistance, then you must do this together with your spouse.

Do not allow anyone to speak ill about your spouse in your presence. Nobody should feel comfortable speak ing about your spouse in a negative manner in your presence. You may have to set boundaries with your family and friends to make sure that respect for your spouse is always maintained. If somebody speaks about your spouse in a negative manner in front of you, you must defend your spouse immediately.

Do not tell each other's secrets. When your spouse entrusts you with something, it is important that you do not break their trust. Once trust is broken it is very difficult to regain. Your spouse will confide in you about precious matters and it is your duty to keep those matters private. Breaking the trust is also a great sin before Allaah.

If any of you have been previously married, it is important not to compare your new spouse to your ex. Do not make any comparisons, even jokingly. You must also never praise or compliment that ex-spouse in the presence of your new spouse.

Avoid being stingy with your money. Financial matters are rarely spoken about when it comes to marriage in Islam. However, financial compatibility is very important to a successful marriage. It is not about being rich, rather it is about understanding each other. Do not be hesitant to spend on your wife and your family. Remember that spending on your family is considered charity. It was reported by Abu Mas'ud [R.A] that the Prophet [S.A.W] said "When a man spends on his family and hopes to be rewarded for it, it is a charity for him." Sahih Bukhari 55.

It was also said by Ibn Kathir that "It was the character of the Prophet to live in a beautiful manner with his wives, being cheerful and kind to them, generously spending on them, and laughing with them." Source: Tafsīr Ibn Kathīr 4:19.

Do not make your love for each other to be conditional. This means that you must not wait for your spouse to do good to you first before you do good for them. This will make the actions to be insincere. You should love each other for the sake of Allaah and be good to each other for the sake of Allaah.

* * *

19. Questions

Questions To Spark Conversation And Form Connection

1. Who is the most inspiring person you know today?
2. Has your life turned out the way that you expected it to?
3. What would you change about the way your parents raised you?
4. What would you say is your best physical feature?
5. What would you say is my best physical feature?
6. What would you say is your best personality trait?
7. What would you say is my best personality trait?
8. Tell me something that I don't know about you?
9. Tell me the top two happiest moments in your life?
10. Tell me the top two saddest moments in your life?
11. If you could change one thing from your past, what would it be?
12. What is your favourite memory with me so far?
13. What are you most grateful for in your life?
14. If you could go back 10 years, what would you say to yourself? Three words only.
15. If you could relive a year in your life, which age would you choose?
16. What do you consider too serious to be joked about?
17. In which ways are we similar?
18. Summarise your life story for me in two minutes.
19. If you could wake up tomorrow having achieved one thing, what would It be?
20. How close-knit is your family?
21. When did you last cry alone? and in front of another person?
22. Name one way that we are different ?
23. When do you most feel loved by me?
24. Name one thing that you are glad you'll never have to do again?
25. What would be your perfect romantic night?
26. When did you first realise that you loved me?
27. If you could change one thing about your looks, what would it be?
28. If you could live anywhere in the world for a year, where would that

be ?
29. Are you more similar to your mother or father?
30. Name three highlights of your life so far.

* * *

Afterword

Marriage has been decreed by Allaah as a mercy and a blessing for us. Allaah says in the Glorious Qur`an "And among His Signs is this, that He created for you mates from among yourselves, that ye may dwell in tranquillity with them, and He has put love and mercy between your (hearts): verily in that are Signs for those who reflect."

Marriage is a place to feel safe to love and to be loved deeply. When you marry someone, you derail them from the life that they were living and you bring them into your life - It is incumbent upon you to ensure that the new life that you begin with them is better than what they have left behind.

Be prepared to change and compromise on things that you may never have expected to. Marriage is *supposed* to change you, It is supposed to make you a better person. If your marriage is not helping you to become a better version of yourself and to become closer to Allaah, then know that something is terribly wrong.

As you conclude this book, we hope that you have realised that marriage is a truly valuable thing. We hope that you have learned that marriage requires daily maintenance in order for you to get the best from it. And last but by no means least, we hope to have ignited hope in your heart that it is possible to attain a marriage that is full of love and true connection.

Asalam alaykum wa rahmatullaahi wa barakatuh

✽ ✽ ✽

SECURE THE KNOT

Printed in Poland
by Amazon Fulfillment
Poland Sp. z o.o., Wrocław
29 August 2023

62eff45c-56e9-464f-936d-e6c6ef544d7cR01